The Ethics of William James

The Ethics of

WILLIAM JAMES

Bernard P. Brennan

BOOKMAN ASSOCIATES :: New York

TO MY COLLEAGUES
AT
PACE COLLEGE

Contents

Introduction

Since James never published a systematic exposition of his views on ethics, any attempt to understand his moral thought requires, first of all, the construction of an outline of his ethical views, synthesizing the moral implications of his statements on metaphysics, religion, and epistemology, and, of course, his statements on explicitly ethical topics.

A systematic exposition of James's ethics is especially challenging in view of the kind of superficial statements that one sometimes hears to the effect that pragmatists have "no ethics" or that their ethics "justify" absolutely anything that is *useful* to the person involved. In effect, these views present a reason for investigating the possibilities of constructing an ethics within the framework set up by one type of pragmatism and a reason for examining the actual meanings of the word *useful* as it is employed by James in connection with his ethics. Finally, such statements seem also to provide a good reason for studying the ethics which James actually works out in connection with his pragmatism, pluralism, and Radical Empiricism.

As we examine James's ethical thoughts, we shall discover that any systematic exposition predominately in terms of one or two of his principal angles of vision, to the exclusion of others, will produce a distortion that is utterly false to James's general intentions. Thus, his anti-intellectualism, his romanticism, his voluntarism, his hatred of monism, his deep-rooted pluralism, his Radical Empiricism, and his pragmatism must be seen always in the general framework of his thought and in their relationships with one another. By itself, no single point of view provides the key to his thought.

The principal source of information for this study has been, as one might expect, James's own writings. Among these, the most valuable are *The Will to Believe,* which affirms the basic importance of moral questions and affirms also the existence of morality; *A Pluralistic Universe,* which develops an ethics-oriented metaphysics; *The Principles of Psychology,* which supports James's effort to find an objective basis for ethics by introducing the doctrine of necessary ideas; and *The Varieties of Religious Experience,* which concludes that Christian sainthood embodies the highest morality which man has yet attained.

For advice and encouragement in the writing of this book I am grateful to my friends, Mr. Vincent Garahan and Professors Quentin Lauer, John Flynn, Bryce Thomas, and Robert Pollock.

B. P. B.

Pace College
New York City

The Ethics of William James

I

The Existence of Morality

Before we examine in detail the moral implications of James's philosophy, it would be well to ask whether his pragmatism does not rule out, from the very start, any possibility of morality properly so called. Is it true that James's so-called morality is at best an endorsement of mere expediency, a code whereby each individual may legitimately do whatever he believes will best advance his own interests, regardless of the consequences, good or bad, which may accrue to other persons? This viewpoint is not without its adherents; at one time, for example, it was the view of Benito Mussolini, who claimed James as one of his philosophical masters. Declaring that James's pragmatism was of great use to him in his political career, Mussolini praised it for teaching him that "an action should be judged rather by its results than by its doctrinary basis."[1]

As a matter of fact, however, the moral views of James are much too complex to be reduced with any degree of fairness to any single formula. Moreover, as we shall see, James was vitally concerned with the construction of a system of ethical ideals which would not be equated with the so-called "ideals" of the "strong man." As we shall show, the Christian saint, with his renunciation and self-sacrifice and charity, embodies the highest moral ideals of James's pragmatism; Nietzsche's representation of saints as degener-

ates *par excellence* and men of insufficient vitality, is not
implied at all in James's pragmatism.[2]

As a matter of fact, the philosophy of William James may
be fairly viewed as a passionate and articulate protest against
the dominant current of materialisms and rationalisms, a
protest made often on behalf of moral beliefs. In the name
of science, in the name of religion, and in the name of
humanity, James affirmed, over and over again, the real
existence and the intrinsic importance of morality.

Pragmatist though he was, James, in his utterances on
the nature of morality, generally avoids what has been
called the "narrowing and accidental reductions which the
pragmatic outlook imposes upon our approach to being."[3]
As a matter of fact, James carefully avoids most such reductions with respect to morality. Of him we cannot say
that he "takes it for granted that everything which is accessible to our immediate experience is doubtful, subjective,
or at best only a secondary aspect of reality which cannot
demand or win our full attention and interest."[4] Denying
the alleged superiority of the inorganic over the organic,
he demanded that all data, subjective or otherwise, be given
a full hearing on terms compatible with their possible
autonomy and reality.

In the data of experience he discovered some data which
corresponded to the realm traditionally called moral. These
data, he affirmed, were true realities in every sense of that
word. He saw man's chief difference from brute animals in
the "exuberant excess of his subjective propensities";[5] and,
in insisting over and over again that "the aim and end of
every sound philosophy" is behavior,[6] he stressed not only the
reality of morality but the primacy of its role in philosophy.
Men, he said, who were ascertaining the moral character
of being were engaged in an almost infinite speculative task.

The moral interest of James continued in his seeing the
final purpose of creation as being most plausibly "the great-

est enrichment of our ethical consciousness."[7] The drama of the cosmos exists for moral purposes; its most significant events are those that are morally relevant.

To enter into an objective philosophy of things, he said, we must take the yoke of moral duty upon our shoulders, "regard something else than our feeling as our limit, our master, and our law; be willing to live and die in its service."[8] We can come to *know* moral truths only by *doing* them; such truths cannot exist abstractly, that is, apart from some concrete consciousness, and they can be known only when they are actualized in concrete human experiences.

Being thus thoroughly convinced not only that morality is completely real but also that the primary object and goal of philosophy is behavior, James believed that some kind of moral system and subordination must exist. He saw that as long as a philosopher holds to the hope of having a philosophy, some ideals must be believed to have "more truth or authority" than other ideals and that to these "the others ought to yield."[9]

In the process of exploring moral phenomena, man must consider his own subjective interests: "To bid the man's subjective interests be passive till truth express itself from out the environment, is to bid the sculptor's chisel be passive till the statue express itself from out the stone."[10] Man's subjective desire to have a genuine ethical universe is a *sine qua non* for the "discovery" of that universe—just as is the scientist's subjective desire for a simple, consistent, coherent account of the world a prerequisite for the development of science. In both cases the human subjective interests are legitimate elements. (In the chapter on epistemology and morality we shall consider in more detail this creative role which man plays in his relationship to truth and the moral implications of this role.)

In following his desire to have a morally unified universe, the moral philosopher must take the ideals which he finds existing in the world and see how they can be got into a certain form. In doing so, however, the philosopher must avoid the "superstition" of believing in a system of moral relations which are true in themselves (unless the philosopher happens to be a theist, who can place the code in God's mind).[11] He must avoid ethical philosophies dogmatically made up in advance; he must avoid the temptation to suppose "that our demands can be accounted for by any one underlying kind of motive," realizing that the "elementary forces in ethics are probably as plural as those of physics are."[12]

Having no common character apart from the fact that they are ideals, "the objective validity of moral ideals is lodged in the *de facto* constitution of some existing consciousness."[13] Without an actual consciousness, goodness, badness, and obligation could not be realized. But wherever such actual living minds do exist "with judgments of good and ill, and demands upon one another, there is an ethical world in its essential features."[14]

These judgments in moral matters are of utmost importance, so much so that scepticism in such matters is really "an active ally of immorality . . . The universe will have no neutrals in these questions."[15] If we become epicureans we shall have a world view that regards the world as being "of fundamentally trivial import"; if we become moralists we shall see the nature of things as being "earnest infinitely."[16]

As we shall see, morality plays a major role in the pragmatism of James. Service in the ranks of morality is a kind of "cosmic patriotism";[17] for James the "power of moral or volitional response to the nature of things will be the deepest organ therewith we shall ever possess."[18]

II

Metaphysics and Morality

One of William James's lifelong desires was to publish a definitive statement of his metaphysical views; he cherished, as Henry James, Jr., says, "the purpose of stating his views on certain problems of metaphysics in a book addressed particularly to readers of philosophy."[1] This purpose was, unfortunately, never achieved. We have, however, a fragmentary and incomplete formulation in the posthumously published volume *Some Problems of Philosophy*; in addition, of course, there are many metaphysical observations scattered throughtout other writings. These metaphysical views illuminate in a most meaningful way the moral implications of his philosophy.

In this chapter we shall try to explicate the relationships between metaphysics and morality as they are generally viewed by James.

The first point that we wish to make is that this relationship, as Schneider has noted, involved the subordination of metaphysics to ethics,[2] a fact reflected in James's oft-repeated dictum that behavior is the goal of philosophy.

However, before exploring this relationship in detail, we should note that we can find in James's writings contrary statements which seem to make ethics subordinate to metaphysics. For example, in "The Moral Philosopher and the Moral Life" James says, "The chief of all the reasons why

17

concrete ethics cannot be final is that they have to wait on
metaphysical and theological beliefs."[3] Regarding this statement, however, we note that it refers specifically to the
priority of metaphysics and theology over *concrete* ethics;
the reference apparently is not meant to include general
moral principles. Moreover, the exceptional character of the
statement can be demonstrated by many quotations ex-
pressing the opposite viewpoint, for example, this one from
"The Sentiment of Rationality": "We demand in it [the
universe] a character for which our emotions and active
propensities shall be a match."[4] It is more to the point, therefore, to say that the universe must fit man's needs[5] rather
than say that man's needs are not relevant in determining
or revealing the nature of the universe. In our own cravings
we may have one of the very best clues to the nature of the
world.

Indeed, the test of the satisfactoriness of a philosophy,
according to James, consists in seeing whether or not it
contradicts our active propensities; a philosophy must not
deny "reality to the objects of almost all the impulses which
we most cherish."[6] Philosophy must not assume that reality
cannot or will not be truly akin to our subjective tendencies;
it must avoid the naive assumption that our subjective life
is actually alien and inferior to external reality.

Accordingly, if we were to set science up as the *causa ex-
emplaris* for all philosophy, we should be especially careful
to avoid the common unphilosophic presupposition that
science's objectivity is based upon the fact that science is free
of all subjective human desires and goals. As we shall see
when we examine the relationships between epistemology
and morality, the purely human, subjective elements which
are really prerequisites of science are vast and indispensable.[7] This is true also of philosophy.

That this personal element is central in philosophical
studies James declared as early as 1879: "It is almost incred-

ible that men who are themselves working philosophers should pretend that any philosophy can be, or ever has been, constructed without help of personal preference, belief, or divination."[8] Personal preferences include not only intellectual interests but also non-intellectual interests. (Without some interests there can be no truths, moral or otherwise.) [9]

From the very outset, a philosopher must take into account these important human interests and demands; in developing his philosophy he must know these very interests and demands and must conform to them in his philosophical views. James's own philosophical work is always governed by a desire to conform to man's basic moral drives and interests.

Bearing this desire in mind, we can understand better the moral significance of Radical Empiricism and pragmatism; by evolving a philosophy which was both pragmatic and radically empirical, James hoped to provide the best possible philosophical milieu for morality.[10] While these two components, Radical Empiricism and pragmatism, are distinct elements, they are also so deeply interrelated in his exposition as to re-enforce and guide each other.

This interrelationship, however, is not such that Radical Empiricism could not logically exist without pragmatism or pragmatism without Radical Empiricism. In his preface to *Pragmatism* (1907), James declares: ". . . there is no logical connection between pragmatism, as I understand it, and the doctrine which I have recently set forth as 'radical empiricism.' The latter stands on its own feet. One may entirely reject it and still be a pragmatist."[11] The same distinction is made in a letter to Theodore Flournoy, wherein James requests him to be careful "to distinguish in my own work between the pragmatism and the 'radical empiricism' . . . *which to my mind have no necessary connexion with each other.*"[12]

In general, we may say that James regards his pragmatism as a *method* in philosophy (and, by extension, a *theory* of

truth[13]), while, on the other hand, he considers Radical
Empiricism to be a *metaphysical doctrine*. James came to a
prise de conscience regarding pragmatism long after he had
settled upon Radical Empiricism as his metaphysics; his own
general understanding of pragmatism is such that it remains
logically distinct from, though conjoined with, Radical
Empiricism.[14]

Thus, statements which seem to imply that somehow
James's pragmatism and Radical Empiricism are necessarily
identical must always be read in the light of his own explicit statement to the contrary. Accordingly, we should
read this statement by Dewey as an expression of intimate
affinity rather than identity: ". . . James . . . repeatedly
stated that pragmatism is merely empiricism pushed to its
legitimate conclusions."[15] Likewise, Peirce's statement: "The
famed psychologist, James, first took it [the word *pragmatism*] up, seeing that his 'radical empiricism' substantially
answered to the writer's [Peirce's] definition of pragmatism,
albeit with a certain difference in the point of view."[16]

There is an affinity, a "complementariness," between
pragmatism and Radical Empiricism which make them
appear almost identical. Yet, in our discussion we must
follow James's request to distinguish between them, regarding, if we wish, James's pragmatism as "the vestibule of his
radical empiricism."[17] Whatever else it may be for other
philosophers, pragmatism is, for James, primarily a method
in philosophy and a theory of truth.[18]

To appreciate the significance of Radical Empiricism for
James, we must understand his interest in philosophically
validating the experiences which constitute the moral life
of man and see that this interest leads him away from the
"vicious intellectualism" of the absolutists (because they
dissolved moral entities in their abstractions) and also away
from traditional British empiricism which veered towards
positivism and the atomization of experience.[19]

It was James's belief that the only way to know reality and at the same time validate moral experiences is to look away from the works of the philosophers and examine human experiences themselves. The philosopher must take experiences as the roots of philosophy, as its very fabric and structure; without—so far as humanly possible—imposing *a priori* conditions for the acceptance or rejection of experiences, he must accept all parts and all kinds of experiences as being philosophically significant. This acceptance of all kinds of experiences distinguishes him from idealists as well as from the British empiricists who are actually only "half-hearted" in their empiricism.[20]

Philosophy must indeed be empirical in the most radical manner. To know reality, man must plunge into his experiences. He must accept and respect sensational life; see relations of time, space, difference, likeness, change, rate, cause, etc., as integral members of the sensational flux; see that the essence of life is its continually changing character; respect his own vital functions, for example, his enthusiasm; and see that only concrete things exist. He must respect *all* the facts of man's moral and intellectual life; on all levels he must accept *all* data, ranging from the concrete physical perceptions to the specific "necessary truths" which are given to him in his various mental, moral, and aesthetic experiences. In this way his empiricism will be truly radical.[21]

Radical Empiricism accepts not only the reality of physical facts but also the reality of thought, which it views as being itself "a most momentous part of fact."[22] Although it rejects "vicious" abstractionism, Radical Empiricism does not fail to perceive that concepts are real beings: "Concepts are thus as real as percepts, for we cannot live a moment without taking account of them."[23] Moreover, it affirms, contrary to the older British empirical viewpoint, that the conjunctions which we experience are as real as the disjunctions.[24] Indeed, we see that Radical Empiricism stresses the necessity of accepting all types of experiences as philosophically significant. Everything which is given is significant. Only by burying himself "in the thickness of passing moments"[25] can a man come to know the inner nature of reality.[26]

Negatively stated, Radical Empiricism postulates that philosophers shall not debate about things which are not "definable in terms drawn from experience."[27] This means that philosophers must not trouble themselves about alleged trans-empirical realities. (With reference to our subject, we see that moral data, experienced as they are by man, are proper subjects for philosophical study. Indeed, they are as fully entitled to serious consideration as any other experiences. The Radical Empiricist must take the existence of moral data as facts of experience; such data will have exactly that kind of reality which experience reveals.)

For Radical Empiricism, the reality of moral data is such that it requires no extra-experiential supports. Having once been experienced, moral data, like all other experiences, must be regarded as entirely "self-supporting."[28] Radical Empiricists must accept the fact that at some point no further explanations of experiences can be discovered; they must accept this fact without feeling 'that' they are obliged to choose between rejecting a given experience or devising some intellectual moorings for it, moorings beyond the ken of man. They must have the courage to let their experiences stand on their own feet, and allow being to "breast nonentity."[29]

Thus, if man has experiences in the moral realm, Radical Empiricism must admit them as being real. If the philosopher finds that he can discuss such experiences and organize them within the general context of experience, he should do so. But, on the other hand, he must resist all tendencies to give his expositions a "higher" rationality by referring them to *trans-empirical* foundations, goals, or hierarchies.

Like all other realities, morality must have its existence in experience itself, or have no existence whatsoever. Like the rest of reality, morality will have to breast nonentity and can exist only as it grows here and now in our various experiences and in its different specific determinations.

For James, all philosophical opinions must satisfy a basic empirical test: Theories must be based upon data which are experienced by men in their internal or external life; they must conform to those realities which call for acknowledgment within a total human life. Alleged realities must be such that they remain within the process of experience.

In explicating his views on the nature of experience, James holds firmly to the theory that the world is pluralistic rather than dualistic and the theory that the knower and the object which he knows are one.

If all reality is to be regarded as being composed of experiences, the distinctions between thoughts and objects, between knower and known, are not radical distinctions, and the philosophical problems created by those distinctions are not true problems. Thus when we see that ". . . thoughts in the concrete are made of the same stuff as things are"[30] we understand that the whole orientation towards the problems of being and knowledge must be radically altered by Radical Empiricism.[31]

The relationship between experience in its "pure" state, that is, experience as the immediate flux of life and experience which has been subjected to later reflection with its conceptual categories is a problem which is to be investigated (like other problems) only in so far as such investigation can be pragmatically vindicated. Whatever theories we may evolve about pure experience must be judged—as all other theories are judged—by their success or failure in leading us "back into sensible experience again."[32]

As a matter of fact, experience, as we generally know it, "now flows as if shot through with adjectives and nouns

and prepositions and conjunctions. Its purity is only a relative term, meaning the proportional amount of unver-
balized sensation which it still embodies."[33] Only "new-born
babes or men in a semi-coma . . . may be assumed to have a
pure experience in the literal sense of a *that* which is not yet
and definite *what*, tho' ready to be all sorts of whats. . . ."[34]

In his most mature thought on the nature of experience,
James introduced a distinction between *pure* experience and
subjective or *conscious* experience in order to block the tendency to make *subjectivism* or *solipsism* the only really
admissible synonyms for experience. This distinction he described as follows:

> You seem to think that "experience" means necessarily
> *subjective* experience. "Pure" experience for me antedates
> the distinction. It is my name for your ambiguous reality
> from which, wherever conceptually developed, the two sets
> of data come. It is not an "ultimate" in the sense which
> you [Warner Fite] condemn. Its determinations are all
> retrospective, drawn from what it develops into . . . it is a
> dualism *in posse*.[35]

With respect to our own lives, we find that reality, no
matter how remote it may be, is always to be defined as
"a terminus within the general possibilities of experience."[36]
Given to us in the form of a "solid plenitude of facts,"[37]
this reality is not to be taken and preserved in its given form.
"It [the given order of experiences] is an order with which
we have nothing to do but to get away from it as fast as
possible. As I said, we break it: we break it into histories,
and we break it into arts, and we break it into sciences; and
then we begin to feel at home."[38]

Our relationship to reality, then, is such that we take a
dynamic and creative role in organizing the world and our
knowledge. Being ourselves vital parts of the total reality,
we play (and rightly so) roles of vast importance in the

"begetting" of the order of the world. In this connection, we act rightly when we accept all experiences as they are given to us, without imposing narrowing, preconceived ideas as to what reality should consist of. Out of this totality of experiences which the Radical Empiricist says we *must* accept as *real*, we then select and organize those which prove on a pragmatic basis to be such as to promote human life at its best. The way in which we do this with reference to our metaphysical views is the subject of the present chapter; how it is done with reference to religion, epistemology, and the moral life of man is the subject of the chapters which follow.

Pure experience obviously starts with the immediately given. This immediately given comes to us in the form of "biography." "Biography," says James, "is the concrete form in which all that is is immediately given; the perceptual flux is the authentic stuff of our biographies. . . ."[39]

In the pulse of our inner life immediately present now in each of us is, he observes, "a little past, a little future, a little awareness of our own body, of each other's persons, of these sublimities we are trying to talk about . . . of truth and error, of good and bad, and of who knows how much more?"[40]

The immediate data of experience, taken, as they should be, at face value, present a vast array of relationships. Among these are conjunctive relations which have every bit as much reality as disjunctive relations (despite the insistence of Positivism to the contrary). Such conjunctive relations must be admitted in our philosophic constructions; their significance for the moral life of man will be seen to be vast indeed.

Having accepted the immediate data of experience as real, we set to work to organize them. Ideally, we should organize them into shapes that will be pragmatically rewarding in the highest degree (see *infra*). In this process, the

masses of beliefs which we already possess will play a great
part in the assimilation, rejection, and arrangement of our
unorganized pure experiences. All of these beliefs, including
those "common-sense traditions" which we received from
our predecessors, must have been themselves originally based
upon experiences; if they had been derived from anything
other than experience, they would have no validity, that is,
they would neither lead us back to concrete facts in our own
experience nor help us deal fruitfully with the problems of
life. (The funded knowledge of the human race must be
governed by the same principle that rules in our own personal discoveries: it must be firmly grounded in human
experiences. Valid traditions serve to put experiences into
a more shareable and manageable shape.)

The unformed character of the simply given order which
is presented in pure experience has turned out to be highly
responsive to human desires and interests. This can be
demonstrated particularly by referring to the reshapings of
experience that give rise to mathematical and physical
sciences. Resolved to cast the world into "a more rational
shape in our minds than the shape into which it is thrown
there by the crude order of experience," we find the world
"plastic to this demand of ours for rationality."[41]

The pragmatic triumphs of the physical and mathematical sciences prove the validity of these reshapings of the
given order. Such plasticity to the subjective demands of
man for special types of consistencies (which, after all, are
what constitute the sciences) is not to be restricted only to
"scientific" demands. The moral longings of man, which are
every bit as real in experience as his longings for physical or
mathematical consistencies, do, we may believe, play equally
valid roles in his reshaping of the simply given. Both ethics
and the physical and mathematical sciences act alike in
choosing, out of the infinite number of relations given to
us, only those that are suited for their own specific purposes.

In calling such relations essential, the moralist and the scientist must each see that they are essential only *for his purpose,* all other relations being as "real and present as they."[42]

A typical, but unusually important question, the answer to which must be forged out of the unformed world of pure experiences, is the basic one, "Is the world a unity or a plurality?" This question, according to James, is the most pregnant of all of the dilemmas of philosophy. Among other things, it has vast implications for morality.

The radical empiricist, of course, insists that one must approach this question by looking at experience. Considering both knower and known as parts of experience, James finds that everywhere there is a perpetual flux. Since reality is identified with experience, he feels that it must possess that "character of qualitative specificity and diversity which is the great and unique contribution of the senses and feeling."[43] Corresponding to the pluralism of experience, the universe itself must be pluralistic, too.

Far from being a world which could be fairly described in monistic terms, the universe of James is radically plural and immeasurably rich in diversity.[44]

Given *this* world, we must examine our experiences of it and see what they reveal about unity and diversity. Actually, we find, for example, in the physical order, that some things are united mechanically, and others divided; some chemically united and others not so united; all physical beings seem to be united by gravitation. "There is thus," says James, "neither absolute oneness nor absolute manyness from the physical point of view, but a mixture of both. Moreover, neither the oneness nor the manyness seems a more essential attribute. . . ."[45]

Since man experiences moral demands for some kind of intimacy with the universe, philosophy must recognize these in constructing a world view. However, instead of conferring

intimacy on man by making him a *partner* in the struggle
for a better world, the monistic view makes him merely a
spectator. Its universe offers him acceptance only on condition that he passively concur in whatever is. Such a "role,"
if inaction can be called by such a name, has, James perceives, an appeal for some people, and only in this way does
monism answer to a limited moral demand.

Although "noetic monism," viewed most favorably, can
possess sublimity, and "shows itself also able to confer religious stability and peace. . . ."[46] still, on deeper consideration, we see that the demand for a monistic universe pro-
ceeds from minds that are morbid. Thus one world view
must be rejected in favor of another because of ethical considerations. The rejected view promotes less noble or more
morbid human conduct, while the approved view is in line
with the truly higher moral demands of the individual. The
credentials of monism are greatly devalued because it fails
to satisfy important ethical demands; thus, the relationship
of metaphysics and morality must be such as will satisfy the
demands of morality.

The need to have a world which responds to our demands
for a moral order is grounds for yet another argument
against monism. The monistic theory must be rejected for
further violating our moral sensibilities by introducing an
unbearable, speculative problem of evil.

If the absolute is, as monists maintain, the source of all
things, and is itself all perfect, how can we explain the
"tremendous imperfection of all finite experience"? Why
should the perfection of the absolute require "just such
particular forms of life as darken the day for our human
imaginations"?[47] These questions are particularly difficult
to answer because the absolute, represented as existing without environment or other beings, cannot have anything
forced upon it. Whatever is, is from the absolute. If the
absolute is good, how can moral and physical imperfections

be explained? This is a question, James says, which absolutists cannot answer, for the ideally perfect whole must have only perfect parts.

Moreover, all attempts to explain the imperfections of the parts as being merely *apparent* imperfections fly in the face of our experiences with evil. Certainly, evil does exist; and, instead of denying its reality, philosophy should accept the existence of evil as being as real as the existence of good.

For the pluralist there is no speculative problem in accepting the fact of evil; indeed the philosopher may provisionally presume that evil facts have "some rational significance."[48] There is even a possibility that evil facts may be "the best key to life's significance, and possibly the only openers of our eyes to the deepest levels of truth."[49]

Thus in their absurd, abstraction-bred fiction of the absolute, monists are forced to choose between introducing an insoluble speculative problem of evil and the equally undesirable necessity of pretending that evil facts do not exist or finally admitting evil into the absolute. The monists' philosophic creed, allegedly supported by the highest kind of reasoning, turns out to be a mere superstition; there is, James declared, no superstition quite like "the idolatry of the Whole."[50]

On the other hand, pluralism, accepting evil facts as real and assigning meaningful roles to them, shows thereby its superiority as a metaphysical hypothesis. For this and other reasons which we shall now investigate, pluralism must be regarded as the only metaphysical postulate adequate to the demands of a moral universe.

Basically, by transforming the nature of the universe from a monolithic whole into a cosmos of related *eaches*, pluralism creates a home for the spirit of man; in a world of absolute oneness, with all events preordained, the active spirit of man could find no scope for action. Instead, foreign to every impulse, a monistic world would call for a fatalism and an indifference which would frustrate the very nature of man. Pluralism, on the other hand, "in exorcizing the absolute, exorcizes the great de-realizer of the only life we are at home in, and thus redeems the nature of reality from essential foreignness. Every end, reason, motive, object of desire or aversion, ground of sorrow or joy that we feel is in the world of finite multifariousness, for only in that world does anything really happen, only there do events come to pass."[51]

Legitimating as it thus does our human hopes and drives, pluralism is to be preferred, even though we can claim for it no more than the status of a hypothesis.

The fact that a pluralistic universe reflects the loosely connected pattern of our daily experience is not at all to be held against pluralism; on the contrary, the theory of a block universe and the prestige accorded to that theory on the basis of its alleged freedom from subjective desires on the part of man are both equally unfounded. As a matter of fact, both pluralism *and* monism are hypotheses constructed to satisfy some purely subjective demands, monism seeking to satisfy the rational demands for consistency, and pluralism the demands for a universe in which man has opportunities to express his moral drives.

Thus, against the absolutist demands that philosophers acknowledge the unique truth of monism, James insists that pluralism must be regarded as "a fully co-ordinate hypothesis with monism." "The world *may*," he says, "in the last resort, be a block-universe; but on the other hand it *may* be a universe only strung-along, not rounded in and closed. Reality *may* exist distributively just as it seems to, after all. On that possibility I do insist."[52]

Of the two possible hypotheses, James chooses the pluralistic largely because it responds positively to his desire for a basically moral universe. "I prefer," he writes, "to stick in the wooden finitude of an ultimate pluralism, because that at least gives me something definite to worship and fight for."[53] And in his introduction to *The Literary Remains of Henry James,* he refers to pluralism as "a view to which we all practically incline when in the full and successful exercise of our moral energy."[54]

This moral basis for James's preference for the pluralistic hypothesis is asserted repeatedly in his writings; for example, in *Pluralistic Universe* he says, "Your relations with it [i.e., a pluralistic universe], intellectual, emotional, and active, remain fluent and congruent with your own nature's chief demands."[55] Insofar as a pluralistic universe satisfies man's moral demands, such a universe must be said to be real. This follows from the Radical Empiricist's belief that all reality equals experience; man's own experiences, including our moral cravings, are the only true key to the universe. Since we have, as a matter of fact, moral experiences, it follows that there *is* morality *in* this world.

The pluralism of James provides room for moral experiences by avoiding that chopping up of experiences into atomistic sensations which characterized Hume's empiricism. While Radical Empiricism affirms that the "each-form" is the eternal form of reality *and* the form of temporal appearance, it does not thereby imply that we have an incoherent "multiverse." As a matter of fact the radical empiricist sees that "every part, though it may not be in actual or immediate connexion, is nevertheless in some possible or mediated connexion, with every other part however remote, through the fact that each part hangs together with its very next neighbors in inextricable interfusion."[56] James's empiricism, accepting the reality of all experiences, gives his pluralism real coherence. In other words, the radical empiricist rejects the naive belief that disjunctions are real while conjunctions are unreal. He accepts the fact of "coalescence of next with next in concrete experience" and acknowledges that all the "insulating cuts we make . . . are artificial products of the conceptualizing faculty. . . ."[57]

While he affirms as his hypothesis that *"reality may exist in distributive form, in the shape not of an all but a set of eaches, just as it seems to be,"*[58] he also declares that pluralism, "pragmatically interpreted, . . . means only that the sundry parts of reality *may be externally related."*[59]

This conditioned independence of the parts which constitute reality introduces the possibility of chance in the world; and our experience shows us that such chance does actually exist. "As ultimate terms, freedom, chance, necessity, truth, fact,, mean one and the same thing—namely *datum* or gift; what (since we find it) we must accept it as having come. . . ."[60]

The moral implications of the real existence of chance are abundantly evident once we consider that only in a world which is incomplete and open to novelty is it possible for man to have freedom.

In his "Syllabus for Philosophy 3," James lists eight reasons in tychism's favor (i.e., in favor of the doctrine of chance or novelty). Of these, three he calls scientific, two moral, and three metaphysical; one of the metaphysical arguments, that tychism eliminates the problem of evil from theology, is evidently moral as well as metaphysical. The two moral reasons are given as follows: "1. Absolutely to deny novelty, as Monism does, and to assume that the universe has exhausted its spontaneity in one act shocks our sense of life. 2. Tychism, essentially pluralistic, goes with empiricism, personalism, democracy, and freedom. It believes that unity is in the process of being genuinely won. In morals it bases obligation on actual demand. Tychism and 'external relation' stand or fall together. They mean genuine individuality, something to *respect* in each thing, something sacred from without, taboo."[61]

James sees that, from a speculative point of view, there is no reason why chance could not be an aboriginal element of the universe and indeed actually form the universe.

common table of space and time"; things, we find, cohere, but in such a way that the act of cohesion "leaves the rest of their qualifications indeterminate."[69]

The hypothesis that determinism is wrong and indeterminism valid is forced on James largely because of moral considerations. In telling why he is not a Hegelian, he states, "The moral judgment may lead us to postulate as irreducible the contingencies of the world."[70]

Crimes, he feels, with all their horror cannot have been called for by the nature of the universe, coming necessarily at appointed times and places; "if nothing else would have been consistent with the sense of the whole, what are we to think of the universe?"[71] Man's sense of morality is violated by the idea that crimes are necessary, and we react instinctively against accepting crimes as being part of the necessary history of the world. These reactions should not be ignored or tampered with; they constitute a judgment against the deterministic hypothesis because, as we have seen, man's subjective reactions are every bit as real and "objective" as any other parts of reality. Therefore, we must hear their testimony. As a matter of fact, they carry greater weight than the alleged truths of monistic intellectualism.

It is precisely his feelings about such reactions that make a man a "possibility" man or an "anti-possibility" man; *not facts but postulates of rationality shape a man's views.* To some, the world seems more rational with possibilities in it; to others, it seems more rational with possibilities excluded. In both cases men are responding equally to subjective demands of their natures; neither side has any right to claim that external evidence favors it, for "facts have hardly anything to do with making us either determinists or indeterminists."[72]

It is possible for James to propose that we should consult our preferences in considering the question of determinism and indeterminism because such preferences, being part of

"The essence of my contention," he says, "is that
where connections are not logically necessary
nevertheless adventitiously '*come.*' Series of indepe.
gin and purpose may inosculate by 'chance-encoun
thereafter mingle their causalities, and combine t
fects."[62]

James's world view, affirming the reality of chan
volves a rejection of the spurious rationality of mo
and looks in "the flux of sensible experience itself"
rationality that has been overlooked.[63] The rationality w.
it finds there is indeed, from the moral point of vi
superior to the "rationality" of monism, which invol
determinism with all its consequences.

This superiority is manifested in the fact that detei
minism, "in denying that anything else can be in its stead,
virtually defines the universe as a place in which what ought
to be is impossible."[64] Thus, determinism, or monism, imposes upon the universe a character which we find morally
repugnant as well as self-contradictory; in doing so in the
name of greater rationality or greater perfection, all monistic, absolutist, and deterministic world views reveal their
utter irrationality.

On the other hand, Radical Empiricism, positing a finite
world in which change and chance play a part,[65] gives us a
world such that "all the categories of my sympathy are knit
up" with it,[66] a world made up of "eaches" allowing us
"the highest degree of intimacy."[67]

As we investigate this world, gathering philosophic conclusions from the particulars of life, we come to see that
"chance, the very name of which we are urged to shrink
from as from a metaphysical pestilence, means only the
negative fact that no part of the world, however big, can
claim to control absolutely the destinies of the whole."[68] We
find it deeply probable that "all the qualities of being
respect one another's personal sacredness, yet sit at the

man's experiences, are as real as any other data. Exploring
such areas of human experiences—without being hampered
by rationalistic or positivistic prejudices against them—James
finds that they point towards a world which is so constituted
as to give validity to man's moral beliefs and activities.
Our experiences reveal that the individual actually introduces freedom and morality into the universe by affirming indeterminism and by being a good man; on the other
hand, the world itself appears first as a moral nullity ("With
nature as a whole we can establish no moral communion"[73])
and later as a radically moral universe, resting "on an
absolute and ultimate should, on a series of shoulds all the
way down."[74] The relationship of this radically moral universe and the morally good man in an interdigitated whole
plays a major and central role in James's world view.

Although James regarded the world thus as fundamentally
moral, still a few texts can be found indicating that he
seemed to view the universe as amoral or immoral: "To
such a harlot [visible nature] we owe no allegiance; with
her as a whole we can establish no moral communion; and
we are free in our dealings with her several parts to obey or
destroy, and follow no law but that of prudence in coming to
terms with such of her particular features as will help us to
our private ends."[75] "Nature has no one distinguishable
ultimate tendency with which it is possible to feel a sympathy."[76] "If there be a divine Spirit of the universe, nature,
such as we know her, cannot possibly be its *ultimate* word to
man. Either there is no Spirit revealed in nature, or else
it is inadequately revealed there. . . ."[77] "Nature is all plasticity and indifference—a moral multiverse . . . and not a moral
universe."[78]

(The importance which James attached to this question
regarding the morality of the universe is indicated by his
declaration that the "radical question of life" is whether
"this be at bottom a moral or an immoral universe."[79] To

this question James's answer is that the universe *is* radically moral.)

The explanation for the existence of apparently contradictory statements on this point in James's philosophy is simply that the universe *without sentient beings,* or viewed without reference to such beings, is indeed without moral content or relevance, for the reason that moral ideals cannot exist apart from the "de facto constitution of some existing consciousness."[80] If such a consciousness does not exist in the world, then the world lacks any moral character. But once a concrete personal consciousness exists, with its moral ideals, the character of the universe is thereby changed and takes on a radically moral nature. Thus we say that the universe, with man in it or as related to man, is radically moral. The judgments of *better, worse,* and *ought* are as "intimately pertinent to phenomena as the simple judgment *is* or *is not.* . . ."[81]

Now we are driven to a conclusion which makes man, his freedom, and his goodness the moral stuff of the world. If, without man, nature lacks all moral character and if nature can receive moral formation from man, then the universe, morally speaking, will be just what man makes it. "The world *is* good, we must say, since it is what we make it,—and we shall make it good."[82]

The possibility of thus seeing the universe as containing moral dimensions requires us to correct a bad habit in our thinking, the error of "regarding the spiritual not as the rule but as an exception in the midst of nature."[83]

But in light of the following quotation we can see that this so-called solution to the seemingly contradictory, scattered thoughts of James evidently requires further consideration:

> For the absolute moralists, on the contrary, the interests are not there merely to be felt,—they are to be believed in and obeyed. Not only is it best for my social interests to

keep my promise, but best for me to have those interests, and best for the cosmos to have this me. He who believes this to be a radically moral universe must hold the moral order to rest on an absolute and ultimate *should,* on a series of *shoulds* all the way down.[84]

Here we find that the moral order is not the result of our actions, but rests somehow upon something *absolute* and *ultimate.* Do we have here an irreconcilable contradiction, or is there some possibility of making a synthesis of these radically opposed statements? There may well be such a possibility.

By making a review we can recall (a) a stage in which nature is seen as lacking morality, (b) a phase wherein goodness or evil are introduced into the world by men, and (c) an aspect of morality wherein nature is viewed as resting on absolute and ultimate *shoulds.*

All three can be validated and retained within the thought of James in light of this explanation: (a) If one would think of a hypothetical universe without any sentient beings at all, such a universe would be amoral. (b) *Historically speaking,* goodness and evil are introduced into the world by the acts of men. As we have seen, the world, in the absence of any concrete consciousness, is altogether without moral character. Thus, by their good and evil acts men increase the amount of good or evil in the world, and through the course of history, men created the moral character of the universe. (c) *Metaphysically speaking,* however, it is true that the moral order rests on an absolute and ultimate should. In this respect, morality is "independent" of history, just as arithmetic is. (Discussion of this important phase of morality we must defer until the next chapter, when we shall examine the relationship between morality and epistemology, specifically the theory of necessary truths seen as the fruits of experience.)

From the practical point of view (which, for James, is *the* point of view), it is only right James should devote much more of his attention to developing his theories regarding (b), wherein man has an opportunity, through his actions, to determine the moral character of the universe. Thus, too, James gives point (a), very properly, only a little attention, inasmuch as it refers to a purely hypothetical universe; and, finally, he develops the theoretical and speculative basis of ethics, point (c), in connection with his thinking in epistemology and religion.

There seems to be, however, a real problem in relating these points to the existence of the objectively moral universe which James refers to in many passages, such as the following: "If this be an objectively moral universe, all acts that I make on that assumption, all expectations that I ground on it, will tend more and more completely to interdigitate with the phenomena already existing."[85] But how, we may ask, does the existence of an objectively moral universe fit in with this statement: "The world *is* good, we must say, since it is what we make it,—and we shall make it good."[86]

Further thought will disclose that all we need to do to explain this paradox is to rephrase some of the points which we just made, distinguishing, on the one hand, between good and evil as elements historically added to the world by man's actions and, on the other, the moral order as existing independently of history. But, in this new context, we can see that something extra has been added, namely the implication that the historical order (i.e., the deeds done by men) is to be judged in terms of the objective moral order.

If this last statement is a correct interpretation of James's views, then we have arrived at a very important answer to the charge that the ethics of pragmatism were based upon and guided by expediency only.[87]

However, we must go cautiously before we accept this

development as a vindication of James's position because many important details remain to be worked out regarding the very nature of this "objective moral order." And at present it seems that these must be deferred until we have investigated James's theory of knowledge. The exposition of the objective moral order and its basis will, therefore, be the climax of our chapter on morality and epistemology.

Meanwhile, it is possible for us to examine the part played by man in determining the moral character of the universe.

We understand that if man does really play a significant part in shaping the moral character of the universe, then the universe as it exists must be incomplete, real novelties must be possible, man must have free will, and finally man must be able to exercise real causal powers on the world. That all these are all true facts James definitely affirms.

The incompleteness of the world is, of course, an integral part of the pluralistic hypothesis, which views reality as becoming rather than as static being. The pluralist must reject, for example, the intellectualist belief "that our mind comes upon a world complete in itself, and has the duty of ascertaining its contents; but has no power of redetermining its character, for that is already given."[88] The existence of reality in the form of *eaches,* with their various conjunctions and disjunctions, leaves the story of the universe an unfinished one. Its total character can be expressed "only by hypothetical and not by categorical propositions"; its destiny "thus hangs on an *if,* or on a lot of *ifs*" because the world is "as yet unfinished."[89]

This unfinished character of the world means the introduction of novelty, which comes in, as we empirically discover, not by jumps and jolts, but by leaking in "insensibly," as James says, because "adjacents in experience are always interfused. . . ."[90]

Even though no conceptional explanation of how such a

world has come to be is possible, the fact remains that we do "experience novelties all the while. Our perceptual experience overlaps our conceptual reason: The *that* transcends the *why*."[91] We must accept the reality of novelties despite the fact that "vicious" intellectualism, treating the perceptual flux as an illusion, denies on logical grounds the possibility of any changes in the world. We must refuse to rationalize the world conceptually in any way that will *a priori* exclude novelty.[92] What we perceive actually, according to James, is a really growing world, a world which we can conceive as revealing a continuously creative nature.

Not only in nature do we find the entrance of novelty but also in the concrete movements of our soul. In these movements, also, "possibilities, not finished facts, are the realities with which we have actively to deal." "Here [in these movements] is our deepest organ of communication with the nature of things."[93]

As our final word on novelty in the world, we may say that James's most compelling argument in favor of novelty is a moral one: "That 'chance' whose very notion I am exhorted and conjured to banish from my view of the future as the suicide of reason concerning it, that 'chance' is—what? Just this,—the chance that in moral respects the future may be other and better than the past has been."[94] In other words, to believe in chance is to introduce morally desirable elements into the universe; to do so is pragmatically justified in view of the creative role of human beliefs.[95]

In this pluralistic universe, men discover true novelties; not only that, but their experiences disclose that they themselves may determine which of several possible novelties at particular times shall be brought into being. James says, "That we ourselves may be the authors of genuine novelty is the thesis of the doctrine of free-will."[96]

The doctrine of free will fits perfectly into the theory of

Radical Empiricism with its pluralistic universe characterized by chance and possibility. Experience, which is the source of our knowledge as well as the stuff of being, discloses both novelty in the world and freedom in the knower. Thus free will is not "an agent introducing itself into natural processes ab-extra"; it means only "the character of novelty in fresh activity-situations."[97]

The inclusion of free will in the pluralistic universe does not mean, however, that "everything that is physically conceivable is also morally possible. It merely says that of alternatives that really *tempt* our will more than one is really possible."[98] The number of such alternatives, of course, is much smaller than the physical possibilities which we can construct in our imaginations. For example, it is physically possible for an American general to eat his prisoners of war or not eat them, but these alternatives are not likely to call for an act of free will on his part.

Our opinions on both free will and novelty depend upon how we view the problem of causality.

It we should accept the conceptualistic view and affirm the "principle of causality," namely, that the effect in some way already exists in the cause, then "the effect cannot be absolutely novel, and in no radical sense can pluralism be true."[99] Accordingly neither novelties nor free will could exist.

But the intellectualistic approach, butchering our perceptual life in order to make it "comprehensible," has no more claim on our acceptance than has the empirical approach. As a matter of fact, since intellectualism rejects our every moral demand, we are entitled to reject *it* in favor of the more satisfactory hypotheses of Radical Empiricism. Therefore, says James, despite the "vast amount of error in our instinctive perceptions of causal activity,"[100] we are still right in accepting the "vague vision" to which we are brought "by taking our perceptual experience of action at its face-value, and following the analogies which it suggests."[101]

This causal activity, which Radical Empiricism affirms, we ourselves enjoy in our relations with the world. Although it is true that in one sense we are "passive portions of the universe," still, in another sense we show "a curious autonomy, as if we were small active centres on our own account."[102]

Phrased in more grandiloquent terms, we may say that "our acts redetermine the previous nature of the world."[103] And not only do our acts exert causal influences on the world, but also our faith. "It [our faith] may be regarded as a formative factor in the universe, if we be integral parts thereof, and co-determinants, by our behavior, of what its total character may be."[104]

The world which thus responds to our causal influences is neither the best nor the worst of possible worlds. The world, pluralists think, may be "saved on condition that its parts shall do their best. But shipwreck in detail, or even on the whole, is among the open possibilities."[105]

If the world is yet incomplete, it is quite possible that we may be called upon to bear our share in contributing to its future development. "The character of the world's results may in part depend upon our acts."[106] By our behavior the disconnections of the pluralistic universe may be remedied and its defects repaired. "*If we do our best, and* the other powers do *their* best, the world will be perfected— this proposition expresses no actual fact, but only the complexion of a fact thought of as eventually possible."[107]

Our experiences tell us that life is "a real fight—as if there were something really wild in the universe which we, with our idealities and faithfulness, are needed to redeem."[108]

In this fight, the pluralistic nature of the universe permits us to separate the good from the evil, and thus war against evil and nurture the good, throwing our weight on the scales in favor of the emerging moral nature of the universe.

This universe, awaiting our cooperation, is incommensurably superior in a moral sense to one which would be fitted only for "fair-weather human beings susceptible of every passive enjoyment, but without independence, courage or fortitude"; such a Pollyanna universe would fail to elicit from man "every form of triumphant endurance and conquering moral energy."[109]

This world, then, in which we live is a great arena, a battleground, where men are called upon to contribute freely, for better or worse, to the development of that melioristic world which may be made to emerge. Ours is, moreover, probably a world which is "enveloped in a larger world of *some* sort of whose residual properties we at present can frame no positive idea."[110]

Finally, James believes that our world is related to other worlds, from which "higher energies" filter in. He describes this belief in a paragraph in *The Varieties of Religious Experience*: "The whole drift of my education goes to persuade me that the world of our present consciousness is only one out of many worlds of consciousness that exist, and that those other worlds must contain experiences which have a meaning for our life also; and that although in the main their experiences and those of this world keep discrete, yet the two become continuous at certain points, and higher energies filter in. Being faithful in my poor measure to this over-belief, I seem to myself to keep more sane and true."[111]

III

Morality and Religion

Both morality and religion have a common concern with the manner in which we accept the universe; indeed, as James says, at bottom the whole concern of both religion and morality is with this very business of how we accept the universe.[1]

Having this common concern, morality and religion are closely related. Our moral demands play a leading part in the shaping of creeds and cults; our religions introduce possibilities of new depths and dimensions in our moral life.[2]

In examining the relationship between morality and religion, we shall find once again that James gave the primary role to morality. Man's ethical demands lead him to religion. As Bixler observed, ". . . the threads of his [James's] philosophy converge at one point into a defense of religious faith, and . . . *his ethics and his purposive view of human life lead him to a belief in a Deity.*"[3]

As we organize a general outline of James's views, we shall become aware of an interesting paradox. Man accepts religion in the first place because it satisfies some of his most urgent personal desires; but, on the other hand, man can gain the full measure of benefits from religion only by abandoning his concern with his own needs and desires. On pragmatic and empirical grounds, man's acceptance of his paradoxical situation is fully justified. Empirically, man's desires are given in experience; empirically, they are known to be satisfied by religion. Pragmatically, religion is justified because it fills a real subjective need; pragmatically, sub-mission and self-surrender to the calls of the divine are vindicated because they produce in man the noblest and happiest life that man is ever known to have.

While we are thus stressing the interdigitating of morality and religion, we must not fail to see that personal religion embodies "some elements that morality pure and simple does not contain."[4] Religion enriches, and, in the case of Christianity, transforms morality.

The evidence for religion is, of course, entirely *a posteriori* and pragmatic, derived altogether from man's experiences and from necessary truths of experiences. Pointing towards the truth of religion are man's perceptions, desires, and needs, and also an analogy, a "divination" and a postulate.

In his experiences man perceives evidences of a higher being: "something deep down in . . . us tells us that there *is* a Spirit in things to which we owe allegiance";[5] ". . . the believer is continuous, to his own consciousness, at any rate, with a wider self from which saving experiences flow."[6]

These experiences which point to the existence of a higher life in the universe are experiences of a personal, spiritual nature—not *concerned* with the "world." This can be seen from the passages just quoted and from the following lines from *Pluralistic Universe*: "The believer finds that the tenderer parts of his personal life are continuous with a more of the same quality which is operative in the universe outside of him and which he can keep in working touch with, and in a fashion get aboard of and save himself, when all his lower being has gone to pieces in the wreck."[7] "They [believers in religion] have had the vision and they *know*— that is enough—that we inhabit an invisible spiritual envi-ronment from which help comes, our soul being mysteriously one with a larger soul whose instruments we are."[8] Finally, in *The Varieties of Religious Experience*, James writes: "It is as if there were in the human consciousness *a sense of reality, a feeling of objective presence, a perception* of what we may call '*something there*,' more deep and more general than any of the special and particular 'senses' by which current psychology supposes existent reality to be originally revealed."[9]

Man's desires, requiring as they do a spiritual order for their fulfillment, give us a strong pragmatic argument for holding to religious beliefs: ". . . we have a right to supplement it [the physical order] by an unseen spiritual order which we assume on trust, *if only thereby life may seem to us better worth living again*."[10] These desires are grounded on an uneasiness which only religion can solve.

Man, being made uneasy by a belief that there is something wrong about him as he naturally is, seeks a solution by which he may be saved. His salvation is provided by religion, which helps him make "a proper connection with the higher powers."[11]

Belief in religion is reinforced also by the fact that man's needs as they exist cannot be satisfied in the visible world. "And if needs of ours outrun the visible universe, why *may* not that be a sign that an invisible universe is there?"[12] "Not to demand intimate relations with the universe, and not to wish them satisfactory, would be accounted signs of something wrong."[13]

Man's ability to ignore generally the existence of spiritual being is not necessarily evidence against religion. It is quite possible that a spiritual realm might exist, might indeed embrace us, without our being actively aware of such a realm. This possibility is suggested to us "by the analogy of the life of our domestic animals." Just as dogs, for example, are "in our human life but not of it,"[14] so our "whole physical life may lie soaking in a spiritual atmosphere, a dimension of being that we at present have no organ for apprehending."[15]

Pointing also towards a confirmation of religious beliefs in a general way, are a "divination" and a postulate. In speaking of the divination, James says, "Is it not sheer dogmatic folly to say that our inner interest can have no real connection with the forces that the hidden world may contain? In other cases divination based on inner interests have proved prophetic enough. Take science itself!"[16] Along similar lines, men postulate beliefs that affirm religious truths: "They all [the man of affairs, the artist, or the man of science] postulate in the interests of their volitional nature a harmony between the latter and the nature of things. The theologian does no more."[17]

In the last analysis, religious phenomena, like all other data, are to be defended against vicious intellectualistic attacks which reject everything that does not neatly fit into some *a priori* scheme of being. As Perry says, "He [James] started with religion as a datum and held to it until he might justify it for himself."[18] Justification would come in time as James examined concrete religious experiences and found that they aided men in dealing more effectively with their problems.

It was James's belief that in his war against rationalism he was fighting in behalf of religion. He regarded his own brand of empiricism as an ally of religion: "I fully believe that such an empiricism [a thicker and more radical one] is a more natural ally than dialectics ever were, or can be, of the religious life."[19] The pluralistic aspect of his philosophy also can be regarded as an ally of religion. ("It is evident," says Perry, "that pluralism is readily convertible into a philosophy of religion."[20]) Pluralism provides the best possible explanations of such questions as the problem of evil and free will in their relationship to religion.

The religion which emerges from a pragmatic, empirical

approach must, of course, successfully pass a pragmatic test. "The gods we stand by are the gods we need and can use, the gods whose demands on us are reinforcements of our demands on ourselves and on one another."[21]

Rising in the experiences of man, religion is regarded by pragmatism as a *mode of life,* as an element in a life which is an affair of "forced adaptation to an indifferent and, at best, reluctantly plastic environment."[22] Arising from the exigencies of life, religion reflects the qualities of that life, being real, perilous, and doubtful; however, the pragmatic approach, testing religion by the empirical method, leaves religion "in possession of its towering place in history. Economically, the saintly group of qualities is indispensable to the world's welfare."[23]

Nevertheless, religion is not to be identified with, or reduced to, those exigencies of that life out of which it rises. Religious experiences give a set of new facts which could not have been anticipated in advance of their coming. "Reason, operating on our other experiences, even our psychological experiences, could never have inferred these specifically religious experiences in advance of their actual coming. She could not suspect their existence, *for they are discontinuous with the 'natural' experiences they succeed upon and invert their values.*"[24]

This uniqueness of religious experiences makes any materialistic reduction or interpretation utterly impossible. This uniqueness also, introducing as it does totally new elements into our life, makes new demands upon our conduct. The relevance of religion and ethics could not be clearer.

> . . . Religion, in her fullest exercise of function, is not a
> mere illumination of facts already given, not a mere passion,
> like love, which views things in a rosier light. It is indeed
> that, as we have seen abundantly. But it is something
> more, namely, a postulator of new *facts* as well. The world
> interpreted religiously is not the materialistic world over

again, with an altered expression, it must have, over and above the altered expression, *a natural constitution* different at some point from that which a materialistic world would have. It must be such that different events can be expected in it, different conduct must be required.[25]

Seen in the light of religious experiences, the world is wider and richer. These experiences "suggest that our natural experiences, our strictly moralistic and prudential experience, may be only a fragment of real human experience. They soften nature's outlines and open out the strangest possibilities and perspectives."[26]

To recapitulate, we observe that experiences point beyond themselves "to a realm that no human eye has yet seen—an empirical realm, of course, but one that you have a right to interpret in terms of a faith that is itself active, but that is not merely worldly and athletic."[27] This realm, once it is embraced through faith, transforms the world we know, introducing new values and placing new demands on our conduct of life.

The transformation of the world by religion comes about by adding two postulates of profound moral significance to the postulates of science and morality. To the postulate of science, that things *are,* and to the postulate of morality, that some things are *better* than other things, religion adds, first, that "the best things are the more eternal things"[28] and, second, that "we are better off even now if we believe her [religion's] first affirmation to be true."[29] When the mind accepts these affirmations as true, we find that our experiences are "enveloped in an eternal moral order" and our sufferings have "an immortal significance";[30] we then pass our days with zest, stirred by prospects, thrilled by remoter values. We find ourselves assured of "safety and a temper of peace, and, in relation to others, a preponderance of loving affection."[31]

Religion brings to us increased powers of moral vision and profound moral relief. It is the implacable enemy of pessimism, which is itself essentially a religious disorder, springing out of the void which only religion can fill for man.

In the framework of Radical Empiricism James is able to say that religious faith plays a part of great practical importance to man. Tested by pragmatic criteria of truth, religious views, he finds, are true. Conversely, pragmatism and Radical Empiricism are in turn validated by the fact that they satisfy man's practical needs by providing a place for religious demands in our philosophy of life.

The satisfaction of religious demands involves, obviously, the acceptance of faith and the rejection of scepticism. Man must spurn as absurd the rationalist insistence that religion be rejected until such time as "sufficient evidence" be found. Thus to suspend judgment in the presence of the religious hypothesis is to assume foolishly "that to yield to our fear of its being error is wiser and better than to yield to our hope that it may be true. It is not intellect against all passions, then; it is only intellect with one passion laying down its law."[32] It is the part of wisdom to believe "what is in the line of your needs";[33] for a man's "wants are to be trusted . . . the uneasiness they occasion is still the best guide to his life."[34] Such faith is one of the "forces *by which men live*."[35] The total absence of faith means collapse.

Their influences on man's conduct, their capacity to satisfy man's yearnings, these give validity to religious beliefs; more specifically, "*immediate luminousness* . . . *philosophical reasonableness*, and *moral helpfulness* are the only criteria" required in judging the validity of religious opinions.[36] Beyond this kind of evidence there can be no proofs; "the attempt to demonstrate by purely intellectual processes the truth of the deliverances of direct religious experience is absolutely hopeless";[37] and, indeed, objective certainty can never be added by theological reasoning to a religion that already prevails empirically and answers to the demands of man's moral nature.

However, in thus denying that men can obtain "absolutely incorrigible and unimprovable truth" about the matters of fact with which religions deal, James does not mean thereby to disparage intellectual stability. "Rather do I," he says, "fear to lose truth by this pretension to possess it already wholly. That we can gain more and more of it by moving always in the right direction, I believe. . . ."[38]

Given the living option to believe or not to believe, a man takes a risk no matter how he decides. And regardless of his decision, he takes a leap into the dark, for there is no intellectualistic proof for either scepticism or belief.

But the man who chooses to believe gains by his momentous choice "a certain vital good."[39] Having adopted the practical attitude (not a dogmatic one) which is that of faith, a man ascends to a more enveloping point of view and adopts new rules for action. Beliefs, being chiefly rules for action, give him new scope and dimensions; their truth or falsity are judged on the basis of the conduct that they lead to. A man's religious faith thus "creates its own verification,"[40] a verification in terms of human satisfactions and conduct.

The content of the faiths of various men will vary widely, and it is desirable that this should be so, because religion, being a matter of personal experience, should, in terms of content, vary with different persons. "So a 'god of battles' must be allowed to be the god for one kind of person, a god of peace and heaven and home, the god of another."[41] "Religious thought is carried on in terms of personality, this being, in the world of religion, the one fundamental fact."[42]

While thus holding that a man's personality, his feeling or temperament, play a major role in the shaping and acceptance of beliefs, James states also that feelings and

THE ETHICS OF WILLIAM JAMES

conduct are more constant than religious theories, and therefore provide a more stable basis for religious life.[43]

Regarding feeling, as he did, as "the deeper source of religion," James views theological formulas as "secondary products, like translations of a text into another language."[44] "He [James] found," says Perry, "that the metaphysical and religious speculations which carried men beyond the limits of natural knowledge were inspired by emotion, and must look for their justification to that source. To these considerations is to be added the further fact that James himself *resolved* to allow his subjectivity to color his judgments."[45]

Feelings not only lead us, if we be of congenial temperaments, to religion, but find themselves radically altered once the influences of religion have acted on them. Thus altered, religious feeling is "an absolute addition to the Subject's [sic] range of life," giving him "a new sphere of power."[46]

This religious feeling is of incomparable importance for morality. Coming as an added dimension of emotion, as an enthusiastic temper of espousal, it radically transforms a man's attitudes towards his moral obligations. Where morality without religious feelings could only get him to bow his head and acquiesce, now religion changes hard obedience into joyful participation. Here man arrives at "a new reach of freedom"; the struggle is over, "the keynote of the universe sounding in our ears, and everlasting possession spread before our eyes."[47]

Only under the influence of religion has man achieved his highest moral possibilities; under religious inspiration he takes the yoke of morality and transforms it into a spiritual joy, and exceeds every requirement of the law. "The highest flights of charity, devotion, trust, patience, bravery to which the wings of human nature have spread themselves have been flown for religious ideals."[48]

This transformation takes place, to some extent, in all

religious experiences; but it reaches its highest development in those experiences which are specifically mystical, i.e., religious experiences which are characterized by ineffability, noetic quality, transiency, and passivity.[49]

Having seen that James considers religion and morality to be connected by intimate and significant relationships, we must next ask about the nature of the God or gods whom he assumes as the object of belief. The answer, of course, is vitally important for the explication of his moral views.

In the earliest days of his thought, while he was still a student, James felt that the arguments in favor of naturalism were inescapable and irrefutable; as Perry expresses it, ". . . until he shall discover a saving philosophy for himself he must be peculiarly exposed to naturalistic arguments."[50]

However, after his crisis of 1870, "when the reading of Renouvier gave him the courage to think and believe his way out,"[51] James became an implacable, lifelong foe of naturalism and materialism. His philosophy became and remained essentially religious, his religious views being theistic, but not essentially so.[52] Interpreting James's views on this point, Perry writes, "That religious belief which is at once most probable on theoretical grounds, and most rational in the broader sense of making a 'direct appeal to all those powers of our nature which we hold in highest esteem,' is theism."[53]

Despite the fact that James held to the theistic hypothesis as both probable and pragmatically valuable, he never believed in any coercive rational arguments for the existence of God, maintaining that men believed in God not because of logic but because of their emotional wants.[54] "The divine shall mean for us only such a primal reality as the individual *feels impelled* to respond to solemnly and gravely . . ."[55] It is feeling, rather than demonstrations, which causes us to believe in religion; a feeling, such as that just described, points to an object in which we may believe.

Not traditional rationalistic arguments, such as those of Aristotle, for example, but the actual practical needs of men provide the only bases for validating our belief in God. Such bases or "proofs" may be called "rational" only in the special sense that they are "adequate stimuli to man's practical nature"; and, on the contrary, infra-theistic conceptions, materialisms, and agnosticisms are "irrational" because they are inadequate stimuli to man's practical nature.[56]

Accordingly, the pressures upon us pushing us to a belief in God are not "mental" but volitional, not theoretical but eminently "practical."[57] "Our volitional nature must . . . until the end of time, exert a constant pressure upon the other departments of the mind to induce them to function to theistic conclusions."[58] The evidence for the existence of God, being practical rather than intellectual, is not at all inferior to the rational proofs which were traditionally offered; on the contrary, the ability of the "new arguments" to pass pragmatic tests makes them incomparably superior.[59] If one should test the concept of *God* by the pragmatic method, he would have to reduce it to its positive experienceable operation. Like the concepts *freedom* and *design*, the concept *God* thus reduced means the presence of promise in the world. " 'God or no God?' means 'promise or no promise?' "[60] Thus, pragmatically speaking, the question of the existence or non-existence of God is a meaningful question and one that philosophers must investigate inasmuch as the alternatives suggested imply practical differences which must influence man's actions.

"Her [pragmatism's] only test of probable truth is what works best in the way of leading us, what fits every part of life best and combines with the collectivity of experience's demands, nothing being omitted. If theological ideas should do this, if the notion of God, in particular, should prove to do it, how could pragmatism possibly deny God's existence?"[61]

James believed that pragmatism has a great advantage over both positivistic empiricism and religious rationalism in the religious field. Pragmatism widens the search for God, being willing to follow either logic or the senses and count "the humblest and most personal experiences." "She will count mystical experiences if they have practical consequences. She will take a God who lives in the very dirt of practical fact—if that should seem a likely place to find him."[62]

Following the pragmatic method, one finds the existence of God definitely verified. "On pragmatic principles, if the hypothesis of God works satisfactorily in the widest sense of the word, it is true. Now whatever its residual difficulties may be, experience shows that it certainly does work, and that the problem is to build it out and determine it so that it will combine satisfactorily with all the other working truths."[63] In his examination of data which are personal and particular, James finds that "the drift of all the evidence" seems to him to sweep "very strongly towards the belief in some forms of superhuman life with which we may, unknown to ourselves, be co-conscious."[64] Both Radical Empiricism and faith, adopting the same logical attitude, say that there is "a *plus ultra* beyond all we know, a womb of unimagined other possibility."[65]

In the final analysis, we find that James regarded the religious experience of the individual as "the most authoritative for religion."[66] In examining the total experiences of the individual, we find that the experiences of man which are concerned with the so-called order of nature are only part of man's total experiences. There are other realms of experiences pointing beyond the visible world towards an unseen world of which we now know nothing positive.

This fact which James felt that he had philosophically demonstrated, namely the existence of an unseen world with which man has connections, is of great importance to us in our study of his views on morality. For, as he says, in our relation with this invisible world, "the true significance of our present mundane life consists."[67] The existence of this other world calls for transformation of our ethical theories and our own moral lives.

Among the personal experiences which point towards the existence of a God, James notes the impulse to pray and the tendency of the mind to believe in God. In both cases, there are acts or tendencies of the person such that they call for certain objective realities for their fulfillment; these acts or tendencies are bits of evidence pointing towards the reality of corresponding objects.

"The impulse to pray is a necessary consequence of the fact that whilst the inner-most of the empirical selves of a man is a self of the social sort, it yet can find it only adequate socius in an ideal world."[68]

In two widely separated passages, James refers to God as "the normal object of the mind's belief." In the first instance, he says that an investigation "of the natural history of the mind" shows that God is the normal object of the mind's belief, but adds that "whether over and above this he be really the living truth is another question. If he is, it will show the structure of our mind to be in accordance with the nature of reality. Whether it be or not in such accordance is, it seems to me, one of those questions that belong to the province of faith to decide."[69] In the second passage, he declares that we are forced to regard God as the normal object of the mind's belief "inasmuch as any conception that falls short of God is irrational, if the word 'rational' be taken in its fullest sense; while any conception that goes beyond God is impossible, if the human mind be constructed after the triadic-reflex pattern we have discussed at such length."[70] "My thesis, in other words, is this: that *some* outward reality of a nature defined as God's nature must be defined, is the only ultimate object that is at the same time rational and possible for the human mind's contemplation."[71]

Last but not least, we must mention the moral interests which give pragmatic vindication to a belief in God's existence. In this case, not merely an unseen universe but a living divine thinker is required,[72] and the importance of believing in His existence is stressed by James in a call to pray for the victory of the religious cause: "In the interests of our own ideal of systematically unified moral truth . . . we, as would-be philosophers, must postulate a divine thinker, and pray for the victory of the religious cause."[73]

The world of James is not one made up of matter alone or spirit alone or of both juxtaposed, but rather it is a "value world." Taking experiences as being more than mere appearances, he finds values to be the most fundamental component of the universe. In being loyal to experiences, he is led to take values most seriously.[74]

Upon what we know and believe about the nature of the divine being much of our moral life and ethics is contingent.

For James, the immanence of God has to be stressed, and he feels it necessary to reject all representations of God as omnipotent or omniscient, calling such a God "a disease of the philosophy shop."[75] Many of the traditional beliefs of the great theistic religions are suspect: "The theological machinery that spoke so livingly to our ancestors, with its finite age of the world, its creation out of nothing, its juridical morality and eschatology, its relish for rewards and punishments, the treatment of God as an external contriver, and 'intelligent and moral governor,' sounds as odd to most of us as if it were some outlandish savage religion."[76]

On pragmatic grounds, certain aspects of the traditional theistic beliefs about God are seen to be superfluous and false. James, for example, believes that the traditional God of theism, having once and for all made the world, is known to us through the world and acts on us not directly but through that world. All we need to know, all we need to cooperate with, therefore, is this world; and thus the old theistic God is useless to us and should be discarded. Moreover, the traditional God of theism, living on heights almost as purely abstract as the heights occupied by the Absolute, is "almost as sterile a principle" as the Absolute itself.[77] Existing as a distinct entity, such a God is separated from His creation, leaving the human subject "outside of the deepest reality in the universe."[78] This representation of God mutilates man's religious feelings and therefore must be rejected: "the voice of human experience within us" will judge and condemn "all gods that stand athwart the pathway along which it [experience] feels itself to be advancing."[79]

The prejudices and instincts and common sense which must be our guides reject both a God who absorbs our very being on the one hand and on the other hand a God with whom we can have only external, juridical relations. Such types of deity are abhorrent. The deity of pragmatism must be one and many; "the only opinions quite worthy of arresting our attention will fall within the general scope of what may roughly be called the pantheistic field of vision, the vision of God as the indwelling divine rather than the external creator, and of human life as part and parcel of that deep reality."[80]

The positive belief of James regarding the nature of the deity is both pluralistic and non-dualistic. It is pluralistic because God is viewed as one of the many members of this pluralistic universe, which consists of a multitude of finite beings; it is non-dualistic in that it does not stress the separation between God and the world. Rejecting the older dualistic theism, he rejects also the modern monistic variety of pantheism advanced by the absolutists. The pluralistic pantheism which he espouses affords the intimacy between God and man which he conceives dualistic theism as making impossible; at the same time it affirms "that the absolute sum total of things may never be actually experienced in that shape at all, and that a disseminated, distributed, or incompletely unified appearance is the only form that reality may yet have achieved."[81]

The participation of man and deity in one another's being James explains by a theory which profoundly fascinated him, the theory of panpsychism. There is, he says, "a continuum of cosmic consciousness, against which our individuality builds but accidental fences, and into which our several minds plunge as into a mother-sea or reservoir. . . . Not only psychic research, but metaphysical philosophy, and speculative biology are led in their own ways to look with favor on some such 'panpsychic' view of the universe as this."[82]

Traditional theology, in examining the nature of God, discussed His metaphysical and moral attributes. These now must be tested pragmatically before we can decide whether such attributes lead us closer to God.

The metaphysical attributes, even if we were "forced by a coercive logic to believe them," are "destitute of all intelligible significance"; "how do such qualities as these make any definite connection with our life? . . . Pray, what specific act can I perform in order to adapt myself better to God's simplicity?"[83] The metaphysical attributes must be rejected as irrelevant because James's theology is frankly centered around man, especially man's moral interests.[84]

On the other hand, the moral attributes of God could have real connections with the life of man. For example, "being holy, God can will nothing but the good. Being omnipotent, He can secure its triumph. Being omniscient, He can see us in the dark. Being just, He can punish us for what He sees. Being loving, He can pardon too. Being unalterable, we can count on Him securely."[85]

But, unfortunately, dogmatic theology does not, James feels, really prove beyond doubt that a God with qualities like these actually exists. Once again, only a "trustful sense of presence" in a sincere man upholds the religious faith. "Ratiocination is a relatively superficial and unreal path to the deity. . . ."[86]

Nevertheless, while we reject the doctrines of dogmatic theologians who have explored the divine nature by the use of the intellect, we must not lose sight of the work done in our lives by such concepts as *God, free-will, design,* etc. Referring to these concepts as "dark" in themselves or when "intellectualistically taken," James declares that nevertheless they can have real value "when we bear them into life's thicket with us," for then "the darkness *there* grows light about us."[87] This "ordinary procedure of the religious consciousness" (as Perry calls it) is justified by pragmatism.[88] All that we can say about God is that He has an environment, exists in time, is working out a history; that we must conceive Him as "the deepest power in the universe" and conceive Him under "the form of a mental personality."[89] His personality must be conceived as holding certain things dear; we are right in believing that God is such a being that we and He "have business with each other . . . in opening ourselves to His influence our deepest destiny is fulfilled."[90]

Although it might seem that James's pragmatic theory of truth would make it impossible for him to say very much about the nature of God, he does manage to point out divine attributes which have great significance for man's moral life. In another one of those peculiar two-way situations, we find God's nature deciphered in terms of man's moral cravings and, conversely, man's moral life colored and enlarged by God's interest in him.

With man, God is a co-worker seeking to save the world "on ideal lines";[91] not only do men and God both have purposes for which they care but they also "can hear" one another's call.[92] Sharing the same great cosmic consciousness with God, man finds that by viewing the universe theistically, he changes "the dead blank *it* of the world into a living thou, with whom the whole man may have dealings."[93] Under these circumstances man finds God appealing to his energies and releasing the springs of his emotions;[94] the world takes a turn for the better or worse "as each of us fulfills or evades God's demands."[95]

This need of mankind for active communion with the divine makes absolutistic and deistic constructions abhorrent to James. To the claim, for example, that Spencer's Unknowable was a suitable object of religious faith, James objects: "Mere existence commands no reverence whatever, or any other emotion, until its quality is specified. Neither does mere cosmic 'power' unless it make for something which can claim kinship from our sympathies. . . . As well might you speak of being irreverent to Space or disrespectful to the Equator."[96] But the claim which *God* makes upon us is life answering to life. "A claim thus livingly acknowledged is acknowledged with a solidity and a fullness which no thought of an 'ideal' backing can render complete. . . ."[97] Only a theistic God, therefore, as reinterpreted by pragmatism, says James, can answer to the demands of the human heart. The richest and most satisfying world view must wear such a theistic form.

The God of pragmatism is immersed in the world, doing all kinds of tasks. Unlike the devil, who may be a gentleman, God performs His menial services wherever needed "in the dust of our human trails"; such services on earth are needed more than His dignity is needed in heaven.[98] This presence of God, lending infinite significance to even the smallest details of this world,[99] becomes one of the most powerful motivations in man's moral life.

The man who has a strong sense of the divine will judge and view the visible world in terms of its relations to God: "in its relation to the unseen world the true significance of our present mundane life consists."[100] When a man's affec-

tions "keep in touch with the divinity of the world's author-
ship, fear and egotism fall away," and new vitality enters
into his being.[101]

Although the "exact features of the saving future facts
that our belief in God insures" will not be known until
they have been "cyphered out by the interminable methods
of science" through a study of His creation, still we can
enjoy God "in advance of all that labor."[102] Thus, even at
the present point in man's history, where he knows very
little about God, he can rejoice because the mere notion of
God in itself "guarantees an ideal order that shall be
permanently preserved." The notion of God, for example,
changes tragedy from a phenomenon of a totally evil character to one in which evil may truly be viewed as only
provisional and partial: with God in the world, "shipwreck
and dissolution [are] not the absolutely final things."[103]
"Our attitude towards concrete evils is entirely different in a
world where we believe there are none but finite demanders,
from what it is in one where we joyously face tragedy for an
infinite [*sic*] demander's sake."[104]

The notion of God, furthermore, justifies our moments of
joyousness and carelessness, as we trustfully take a "moral
holiday" in the presence of God.[105] In addition to introducing joy and trustfulness into our lives, a belief that God
exists brings about a wonderful change of perspective in
man's moral outlook: "When, however," says James, "we
believe that a God is there, and that he is one of the claim-
ants, the infinite perspective opens out. The scale of the
symphony is incalculably prolonged. The more imperative
ideals now begin to speak with an altogether new objectivity
and significance, and to utter the penetrating, shattering,
tragically challenging note of appeal."[106]

Here we have in James's philosophy a most eloquent
testimony to the profound and utterly unique role played
by God in man's moral life. Attempts to develop ethical

theories independent of God are always doomed to end in sterility and frustration. Man and his moral life are by themselves incomplete; man, to be fully human, and morality, to flower and bear rich fruits, must find fulfillment in God.

Thus, says James, "even if there were no metaphysical or traditional grounds for believing in a God, men would postulate one simply as a pretext for living hard, and getting out of the game of existence its keenest possibilities of zest."[107] In a human world without God, life would still have a genuinely ethical character, but the full scale of moral values could not open up.

The presence of God in this world of man calls for a response by man which is not made merely by *knowing* about God and acknowledging His existence.[108] Salvation, far from being obtained through gnostic means, is attained only through proper conduct of life. "If religion be a function by which either God's cause or man's cause is to be really advanced, then he who lives the life of it, however narrowly, is a better servant than he who merely knows about it, however much."[109] "To co-operate with his [God's] creation by the best and rightest response seems all he wants of us. In such co-operation with his purposes, not in any chimerical speculative conquest of him, not in any theoretical drinking of him up, must be the real meaning of our destiny."[110]

God's presence in the world has yet another value for man, in particular for ethical philosophers who desire a "stable and systematic moral universe." Only in a world where there is "a divine thinker with all-enveloping demands" can real moral order exist. The way such a thinker subordinates moral demands to one another (if He exists) would be "the finally valid casuistic scale."[111]

When we make the point that a knowledge of God as James visualizes Him transforms man's moral life by enlarging and deepening it, we must also recall that James declares that at any given moment in history man's conception of God is determined largely by the level of morality which has been achieved at that time and place. (A given level of morality serves as a clue to the nature of God.) Thus, the process in which faith is developing is intimately related to the process in which morality is developing. As man's moral life attains greater purity, his knowledge of God in its turn is also purified. "The deity," says James, "to whom the prophets, seers, and devotees who founded the particular cult bore witness was worth something to them personally. They could use him. He guided their imagination, warranted their hopes, and controlled their will,—or else they required him as a safeguard against the demon and curber of other people's crimes. In any case, they chose him for the value of the fruits he seemed to yield. So soon as the fruits began to seem quite worthless; so soon as they conflicted with indispensable human ideals, or thwarted too extensively other values; so soon as they appeared childish, contemptible, or immoral when reflected on, the deity grew discredited, and was erelong neglected and forgotten. . . . When we cease to admire or approve what the definition of deity implies, we end by deeming that deity incredible."[112]

This deity, apprehended so differently by various men, is for Radical Empiricism a "finite" being, one of many members of a pluralistic system. If this belief that God is "finite" is a puzzling one it must be understood in the context of James's thought and not understood in the same sense in which "finite" is used in classical philosophy. James rejects a belief in infinity because he believes that experience gives no indication that there is an infinite being, because he feels that the concept of infinity serves no teleological purpose and because an infinite being must include evil as well as good. But what we should see here is James's intense hope to get God into a most intimate relationship with the world, without identifying Him with it. For him, an infinite being is necessarily completely transcendent, and therefore without any possibility of occupying a place in a philosophy of experience.

The significance of "finite" in this connection is illuminated by referring to James's discussion of the possibility of regarding man's "remote posterity" as a means for awakening the "strenuous mood" in man's moral life.[113] To this suggestion he objects on the grounds that posterity is too "finite," lacking "the note of infinitude and mystery."[114] On the other hand, says he, if man believes in God, he will find that the infinite perspective of moral life will open out. Somehow, therefore, God is more nearly "infinite" than, for example, posterity, without, however, being "infinite" in the classical sense.

God, being thus neither omniscient nor omnipotent, can receive effective support from men in doing His own work. "Who knows whether the faithfulness of individuals here below to their own poor over-beliefs may not actually help God in turn to be more effectively faithful to his own greater tasks?"[115]

The "finitude" of God, as James conceives it, must be accepted as a fact before man can have intimate relationships with the deity, inasmuch as it would be inconceivable to have relations with an "infinite" God. Man's desire for relationship with this deepest power in the universe is one of his profoundest experiences: it points towards, is a clue to, the existence of a being which can give it fulfillment. Such a being cannot be extra-experiential and must not be completely fulfilled and self-contained in its nature.

This being, moreover, must be such in all respects as to satisfy man's moral cravings. (In this respect, the views of James are similar to Whitehead's: "The purpose of God is the attainment of value in the temporal world."[116]) Nothing can be admitted into our conceptions about God's nature if

it will violate our moral experiences. Thus, we must deny
that God is infinite if His infinity violates our moral demands. This, James believes, it does. An "infinite" God
cannot respond to our moral demands.

(To be "finite" is not, for James, an imperfection in
God's nature. His views parallel those of Whitehead, who
sees such finiteness as true perfection: "The limitation of
God is His goodness. He gains his depth of actuality by
his harmony of valuation. It is not true that God is in all
respects infinite. If he were, He would be evil as well as good.
Also this unlimited fusion of evil with good would mean
mere nothingness. He is something decided and is thereby
limited."[117])

When James denies God's infinity, in the traditional
sense of that term, we should be careful not to conclude
that God is seen by him as being relatively unreal and
unimportant. With his finitude (and, to James's way of
thinking, because of his finitude), God has great reality and
the highest degree of importance. He is the deepest reality,
and, with his finite nature, is related most intimately with
all things in the world, particularly with man. He elevates,
enlarges, and transforms man's moral life; the religious emotion itself is such that it renews life: ". . . this emotion
overcomes temperamental melancholy and imparts endurance to the Subject, or a zest, or a meaning, or an enchant-
ment and glory to the common objects of life."[118]

Thus, we see that the theory that a finite God "gains" by
man's cooperation through good works is supplemented by
the belief that man's moral life is dependent upon God.
Man's life and works are seen as being fulfilled by mystical
conformity with God's will; in the final analysis, God is
pictured as having definite moral ascendancy over man, so
that man's happiness consists, not in "using" God, but in
complete and cheerful submission to God. "And here (when
all our mere morality appears vain and provisional) religion

comes to the rescue and takes our fate into her hands. There is a state of mind, known to religious men, but to no others, in which the will to assert ourselves and hold our own has been displaced by a willingness to close our mouths and be as nothing in the floods and waterspouts of God. . . . The time for tension in our soul is over. . . . Fear is not held in abeyance as it is by mere morality, it is positively expunged and washed away."[119]

IV

Epistemology and Morality

At the outset we wish to observe that James's discussions regarding the nature of knowledge *appear* to be less relevant to morality than do his discussions on religion and metaphysics. Furthermore, it might be possible for a general reading of James to lead one to conclude that there are actually very few points of contact between his epistemology and his ethics; indeed, one might simply decide that his epistemology, occupying, as it does, a central position in his thought, cares little about morality.

Nevertheless we believe that by bringing James's epistemological views into focus, with the problems of morality specifically in mind, we can demonstrate the relevance of his epistemology to his ethics. Furthermore, we hope to show that a central concern in his thinking on knowledge, implicitly or explicitly, is to relate knowledge and conduct and to provide epistemological validation of ethical standards of conduct.[1] To do this, we shall synthesize James's views on knowledge, starting with his views on percepts and concepts, moving on to his opinions about objective moral standards and, finally, present his observations about necessary truths and their significance for his ethics.

While our particular arrangement of James's thoughts cannot be found anywhere in his writings, nevertheless we believe it does not violate his fundamental viewpoints.

Quite the contrary, we believe that it is a synthesis which is congenial with his basic interest in ethical inquiries and his desire to see ethical ideals philosophically vindicated.

It is important to recognize the fact that some of his basic views are profoundly original. His terminology, especially his use of the word "empiricism," should not blind us to this originality. As a matter of fact, even though Radical Empiricism does indeed have affinities with British empiricism in general, James himself made clear that he rejected much of the doctrines of Locke, Hume, and Mill. As Perry says, ". . . no modern philosopher has been more alive to the faults and failures of traditional empiricism than he who felt most confident that empiricism was to be the reigning philosophy of the future."[2] For James, the British empiricists were "half-hearted."[3]

Both Mill and Hume, James thought, had succumbed to "that atomistic associationism which was empiricism's family malady."[4] Hume's pluralism made "events rattle against their neighbors as drily as if they were dice in a box."[5] This atomism results, not from empiricism, but from the "intellectualist method" which pulverizes perception and triumphs "over life."[6] This error is not due to empiricism, but rather to a failure to be consistently empirical.

The empiricist's tendency to accept dissociations as being real and associations as being illusory was therefore vigorously rejected by James, who felt that a true experiential philosophy, finding both associations and dissociations in the web of experience, must accept both as real. He regarded Mill's philosophy in particular as derelict in its duties towards the reality of associations; for him Mill's philosophy was "the culmination of that nihilistic tendency in empiricism which sprang from its neglect of unifying relations."[7] In Hume he saw the outstanding example of "the tendency to enthrone mere juxtaposition as lord of all and to make the universe what has well been styled a 'nulliverse.' "[8]

These criticisms of empiricists, however, do not imply a disparagement of the empirical approach. On the contrary, James's criticisms are directed against *poor use* of the method by the men involved. The experiential or experimental approach is quite correct; the failure of Hume, for example, is due to "the poverty of his experientialism" and his blindness to connections, which are "just as unmistakably given as the terms" of experience.[9]

The philosophy of James, then, involves an empiricism corrected and broadened; his philosophy, especially his epistemology, can be understood only in terms of his views about the nature of experience.

Experience, for James, is divided, so to speak, into subjective experience and pure experience. Pure experience is intrinsically neither objective nor subjective, being prior to all distinctions.[10] But James does not clearly and consistently work out the difference between Pure experience and subjective experience. The difference between Pure experience and subjective experience remains, therefore, most difficult to grasp. Actually, experience itself is not dualistic; indeed, as shown in the following quotation, objective experience and subjective experience are only functional attributes of one and the same reality:

> As "subjective" we say that the experience represents; as "objective" it is represented. What represents and what is represented is here numerically the same; but we must remember that no dualism of being represented and representing resides in the experience *per se*. . . . Its subjectivity and objectivity are functional attributes solely.[11]

Important for the epistemologist and the moralist is James's theory that experience itself requires no transexperiential reality as a foundation:[12] in itself, experience is self-sufficient. This self-sufficiency means, of course, that man's mind is not required to seek some being beyond experience in order to attain knowledge. "For pluralistic pragmatism, truth grows up inside of all finite experience."[13] (One may add that truth grows *there*, and *nowhere else*.)

For Radical Empiricism, whatever is real must be contained in our experience; conversely, whatever is in our experience must be somehow "real." This means both that transempirical realities are ruled out and that all experiences, such as those of cause and effect, are included. Against the intellectualists, Radical Empiricism denies the existence of all transempirical being and *a priori* principles;[14] against the "half-hearted" empiricism of Hume it asserts the reality of *all* that we experience. Our philosophy is totally experiential.

Reality itself exists as a *"plenum"*; this *plenum* is "pure experience." But we know as a matter of psychological fact that we cannot experience or think of this *plenum*. Our experiences are at best only fragmentary impressions which are constantly interrupting one another, and our thinking is "an abstract system of hypothetical data and laws."[15]

All that is real is, however, concrete, individual, and universally related by a vast variety of real relationships; all reality is characterized by perpetual processes in which reality grows and takes on new forms. As it exists, reality consists of endless varieties of beings related (not juxtaposed) in an endless variety of ways.

Experience shows us, as Dewey would point out, that things are related, "not as marbles in a box but as events are in history, in a moving, growing, never finished process."[16] In this process pure experience is discovered to antecede the distinction between knower and known, subject and object. Here in being "in the raw" one finds the answer to the great metaphysical and epistemological dilemma which the philosophers have sought to solve in various ways—monism, dualism. Actually, experience reveals a pluralism which has this oné unity, namely the fact that all that is is experience.

While it is true that all knowledge must be *grounded* in experience, it does not follow, however, that knowledge is an unaltered duplication of experience. Neither, on the other hand, does it follow that knowledge is independent of experience. Thus, one cannot call certain "ideals and inward relations amongst the objects of our thought . . . reproductions of the order of outward experience";[17] but, on the other hand, "within experience *itself,* at any rate, . . . some determinations show themselves as being independent of others; some questions . . . can only be answered in one way."[18]

The phenomenon whereby ideals, relations between ideas, and so forth, are added to knowledge independently of experience calls for clarification. If all reality is pure experience and if all knowledge is subjective experience, what can we understand James to mean when he speaks about "the existence, in our thought, of relations which do not merely repeat the couplings of experience"?[19] The only possible answer seems to be that he intends us to understand that internal relations between ideas which do not duplicate external experiences are themselves experienced by us and are therefore as real as any other kind of experiences.[20]

This last observation appears to be borne out in the following quotations (observe the modifiers James attaches to the word *experience,* namely, "passively received experience" and " 'experience' in the ordinary sense") :

> When we pass from scientific to aesthetic and ethical systems, every one readily admits that, although the elements are matters of experience, the peculiar forms of relation into which they are woven are incongruent with the order of *passively received experience.*[21]

But I do not see how any one with a sense for the facts can possibly call our systems immediate results of *'experience'* in the ordinary sense. Every scientific conception is in the first instance a "spontaneous variation" in some one's brain.[22]

To validate the peculiar forms of relation which hold together scientific, aesthetic, and ethical systems, Radical Empiricism must find something in experience which testifies to their existence.

But, in making experience the criterion of truth, James has to face special problems. For example, while it is true that *the order of experience* in some matters (e.g., in the matter of the time—and—space—conjunctions of things) is the real cause of our forms of thought,[23] still in many other cases the forms of our thoughts are not the direct effects of the order of experience. Thus, while it is true to say that "experience moulds us every hour, and makes of our minds a mirror of the time—and—space—connections between the things in the world,"[24] we must nevertheless indicate that the application of this last observation is by no means universal. As a matter of fact, much vital knowledge arises in a fundamentally different way, coming as a result of the mind's reorganization of the crude data of experience.

The fact that there is a type of knowledge involving a reorganization of data by the mind must be stressed over and over again. We must always remember that thought itself, *as a part of experience,* has as much right to consideration as the "crude data of experience." As James says, *"Rather is thought itself a most momentous part of fact,* and the whole mission of the pre-existing and insufficient world of matter may simply be to provoke thought to produce its far more precious supplement."[25]

For the moral implications of James's pragmatism, this aspect of his views of the nature of thought and reality is critically important. Here Radical Empiricism is revealed as possessing enough room to accommodate realities which a narrower interpretation of experience would unfortunately exclude. Among these realities are the data of moral experiences.

In this connection, however, we must point out that there are, on the contrary, some statements which depict mental experiences as being *unreal.* The following is such a statement:

> With "real" objects, on the contrary, consequences always accrue and thus *the real experiences get sifted away from the mental ones,* the things from our thoughts of them, fanciful or true, and precipitated together as the stable part of the whole experience—chaos, under the name of physical world.[26]

On the other hand, many passages affirm the reality of mental experiences, and, in doing so, agree with James's more general views. For example, in *A Pluralistic Universe* James writes, "In the mental world, on the contrary, wholes do in point of fact realize themselves *per se.* The meaning of the whole sentence is just as much a real experience as the feeling of each word is."[27] Here, of course, there can be no doubt that mental phenomena may be real experiences. Experience, both mental and non-mental, provides the standard for judging the truth of all opinions; this standard "grows up endogenously inside the web of experience."[28] Outside of experience there is nothing: if we are going to establish and vindicate morality we must do so with reference to experience and not with reference to standards established in an external absolute. "All the *sanctions* of a law of truth lie in the very texture of experience. Absolute or no absolute, the concrete truth *for us* will always be that way of thinking in which our various experiences most profitably combine."[29]

Thus, for James, experience is not to be judged by logic,

because experience, being *the* only true reality, can be judged only in terms of its own contents. The law of truth which lies in the texture of experience is not subject to the jurisdiction of formal logic. "Reality, life, experience, immediacy, use what word you will, exceeds our logic, overflows and surrounds it."[30]

Subjectively speaking, this reality, life, experience, immediacy, or whatever we call it, is, with reference to our own individual destinies, an "unsharable feeling which each one of us has of the pinch of his individual destiny as he privately feels it rolling out on fortune's wheel."[31] Although this feeling may be "disparaged for its egotism, may be sneered at as unscientific . . . it is the one thing that fills up the measure of our concrete actuality, and any would-be existent that should lack such a feeling, or its analogue, would be a piece of reality only half made up."[32]

This feeling, or pinch, lying at the very heart of our self-awareness, is, as one can readily see, not a specifically intellectual experience. For it, logic cannot be regarded as an adequate definer and confiner of existence, inasmuch as logic itself is a derivative being, while experience itself is the original.

All experiences, however, are subject to correction and reinterpretation. We live, says James, "by the practical faith that we must go on experiencing and thinking over our experience, for only thus can our opinions grow more true. . . ."[33] This necessity to correct and expand our knowledge is imposed on us because of the fact "that all experience is a process," with the result that "no point of view can ever be *the* last one."[34]

While we may regret that experience imposes, so to speak, tentativeness and incompleteness on our opinions, we must also, on the other hand, acknowledge the role of experience as a guarantor against "licentious thinking." "The only *real* guarantee we have against licentious thinking is the circumpressure of experience itself, which gets us sick of concrete errors, whether there be a trans-empirical reality or not."[35] "There are 'bounds of ordinance' set for all things, where they must pause or rue it. 'Facts' are the bounds of human knowledge, set for it, not by it."[36]

Consciousness, the phenomenon in which experiences are known to us, has divided philosophers in their attempts to express what it really is. James regards consciousness as a problem of basic importance and expresses very definite views about its nature.

We know, he says, that consciousness has the form of a "stream" and is not made up of isolated atomic units; we know that the stream of consciousness has two obvious functions, namely, to lead us to knowledge and to lead us to action. We know that *some kind of consciousness is always going on* [in us]. There is a stream, a succession of states, or waves, or fields . . . of knowledge, of feeling, of desire, of deliberation, etc., that constantly pass and repass, and that constitute our inner life."[37]

We know that concrete fields of consciousness are always complex, containing "sensations of our bodies and of the objects around us, memories of past experiences and thoughts of distant things, feelings of satisfaction and dissatisfaction, desires and aversions, and other emotional conditions, together with determinations of the will, in every variety of permutation and combination."[38] We know, too, that the word *consciousness* does not stand for an entity, but rather we insist "most emphatically that it does stand for a function."[39] On the other hand, James declares, we do not know, in any fundamental sense, "where our successive fields of consciousness come from, or why they have the precise inner constitution which they do have."[40]

Perhaps one of the most crucial of James's viewpoints on consciousness is developed in his rejection of Spencer's agnosticism. Rejecting the concept of an unknowable, James insists (as Perry observes) that "consciousness is always cognitive of *something*, and that its critical processes lead to reconstruction rather than to negations of knowledge."[41] Moreover, when consciousness takes the form of the "truth-relation," James, Dewey, and Schiller, all pragmatists, agree absolutely in admitting the "transcendency of the object" to the subject, provided it be an experienceable object.[42] "There is nothing intrinsically unknowable in being."[43]

Far from being directed towards an intrinsically unknowable object or an object that is transcendent or transempirical, knowledge actually has an extremely practical function, namely, to guide man successfully through the real, concrete situations which he faces in this life. This practical point of view is emphasized by James when he recommends the biological approach as having the greatest practical use. This approach emphasizes the fact that "man, whatever else he may be, is primarily a practical being whose mind is given him to aid in adapting him to this world's life."[44]

Instead of viewing knowledge as a unique and particularly God-like kind of reality, James prefers to call it just one element in an organic mental whole, and sees it as "a minister to higher mental powers,—the powers of will."[45] Not only is the cognitive faculty enmeshed in a larger organic mental whole but it is actually incapable of being emancipated from that connection. "Such a thing as its emancipation and absolution from these organic relations receives no faintest color of plausibility from any fact we can discern."[46]

This emphasis upon the practical rather than the theoretical aspects of the functions of the mind is related to specific elements of the theory of evolution. "Man," James says, "we now have reason to believe, has evolved from infra-human ancestors, in whom pure reason hardly existed, if at all, and whose mind, so far as it can have had any function, would appear to have been an organ for adapting their movements to the impressions received from the environment, so as to escape the better from destruction."[47] Man's mind at the present time still functions for the same general practical ends:

> Deep in our own nature the biological foundations of our consciousness persist, undisguised and undiminished. Our sensations are here to attract or deter us, our memories to warn or encourage us, our feelings to impel, and our thoughts to restrain our behavior, so that on the whole we may prosper and our days be long in the land.[48]

The mind is to be regarded as a biologically successful instrument for human survival, developed through the ages by successful confrontation with the difficulties of man's environment. It must be regarded as an *essentially teleological mechanism*.[49]

Although these views are definitely materialistic and naturalistic in their implications, in the wider context of James's philosophy they are made eventually to fit into a spiritual setting.[50] Although the roots are material, we shall see that James wants them to develop spiritual fruit. And, as James says, for his philosophy of pragmatism, it is the results and not the origins that count, whether we are speaking of theories or of practical actions.

In explicating his doctrine of knowledge, James presents us with a picture of the human mind in which its rational element is compelled to work, for the well being of the whole person, in cooperation with the senses and the will. Operating as three "departments," the conceiving, the willing, and the feeling, the mind has for its entire concern the eminently practical goal of human survival and betterment. Since mere sensation and mere conception are inadequate to insure survival of the person, and since only willing can bring about the necessary changes, the pragmatist, in line with his notions about the teleological nature of the mind, must affirm the superiority of the "department" of willing: "perception and thinking are only there for behavior's sake."[51]

For morality, the implications of this theory of the three-department mind are basic and far-reaching. When James has rejected the notion that the theoretic department or faculty should be viewed as synonymous with the mind itself, or that willing and sensation should not be considered parts of knowledge, he opens the way so that he is able to contend that morality does not mean merely conforming to intellectualistic rules, which disregard the whole person.

All theories, moral and otherwise, in this three-department mind must be tested and approved by each and all of the departments. The claims of philosophers that any one department should make solo decisions in the name of the mind must be challenged on behalf of the other departments. The collaboration among the departments guarantees man that his mind will not fail to stick to its work as a *teleological mechanism*.

This doctrine of collaboration, says James, indeed protects pragmatism from certain failures characteristic of other systems of philosophy. Other systems, failing to give due weight to each and all of the three functions of the mind, are doomed to have chaotic philosophies of nature, inconsistent rationalistic metaphysics, and a world view which frustrates the moral demands of human nature.

By what title is it that every would-be universal formula, every system of philosophy which rears its head, receives the inevitable critical volley from one half of mankind, and falls to the rear, to become at the very best the creed of some partial sect? Either it has dropped out of its net some of our impressions of sense,—what we call the facts of nature,— or it has left the theoretic and defining department with a lot of inconsistencies and unmediated transitions on its hands; or else, finally, it has left some one or more of our fundamental active and emotional powers with no object outside of themselves to react-on or to live for. Any one of these defects is fatal to its complete success.[52]

The relationship among these three departments is, as we have seen, not one of equality. As a matter of fact, of the three departments, willing "dominates both the conceiving and the feeling department." Put in plain English, "perception and thinking are only there for behavior's sake."[53]

This dominance of the willing function defines what James means by the teleological character of the mind. Recalling that "the original and still surviving function of our intellectual life is to guide us in the practical adaptation of our expectancies and activities,"[54] we can readily see that the dominance of willing necessarily follows. As a matter of fact, we do not really *know* a given thing, no matter how well we are acquainted with it intellectually, emotionally, and sensibly, unless we know how we should behave towards it. "We are acquainted with a thing," says James, "as soon as we have learned how to behave towards it, or how to meet the behavior which we expect from it. Up to that point it is still 'strange' to us."[55]

We infer, therefore, that we do not *know* God, for example, if we have only theoretical knowledge of His existence and nature; our knowledge is radically incomplete until we have learned how we should behave towards Him and learned also how we should act to meet the behavior which we may expect from Him. The same is true of our knowledge of ourselves, of our neighbors, of social organizations, and even of nature: here, too, emotional or theoretical awareness of beings is not true knowledge until it expands to include cognizance of behavior, until it includes also the willing department of the mind.[56]

The relevance of this doctrine to morality can be explicated by considering the fact that a given moral obligation is not understood, not known, until I see exactly what that obligation means in terms of the behavior that it requires from me. Just as in the case of heat, poverty, the majesty of a sunset, or a long distance to travel—we know these truly only if we have learned how to behave towards them, so also in the case of a given obligation. We do not truly know an obligation unless we know the kind of behavior which it calls for.

Actions of this type, that is, behavior selected in response to the nature of the object known, are actions done for an end, and as such are indubitable expressions of mind. "We impute no mentality to sticks and stones, because they never seem to move for *the sake of* anything, but always when pushed, and then indifferently and with no sign of choice. So we unhesitatingly call them senseless."[57]

While we thus maintain that true knowledge must include an understanding of how we should behave towards various beings, at the same time our own natures demand that reality have, in its turn, a being which is congenial with our own powers and desires. Specifically, we demand that the nature of things should be *rational*; "if it do [*sic*] not seem rational, it will afflict the mind with a ceaseless uneasiness, till it be formulated or interpreted in some other and more congenial way."[58]

This rationality which our minds demand requires more than the satisfaction of intellectual demands in any narrow sense of the meaning of *intellectual*. As a matter of fact, a man actually believes something is rational if he can think of it with "perfect fluency,"[59] or if it "lets loose any action which we are fond of exerting."[60] Rationality is really the absence of any feeling of irrationality; it is the feeling of the "sufficiency of the present moment, of its absoluteness."[61] Philosophies themselves must also be rational in this sense; they must not merely satisfy rational demands and pretend to determine expectancy; they must indeed "in a still greater degree make direct appeal to all those powers in our nature which we hold in highest esteem."[62]

Rationality, in other words, involves more than just logical consistency. To be rational, a theory or an object must satisfy not only the mind's demands for theoretical consistency but also its demands on behalf of its willing and feeling departments. Rationality has "at least four dimensions, intellectual, aesthetical, moral, and practical."[63]

This theory of rationality shows the error involved in demanding that we eliminate the claims of morality and freedom on the grounds that they would violate the logical consistency of the universe. Thus, to sacrifice the notion of personal responsibility, which is so essential a part of the moral dimension of life, to satisfy the demands of the intellectual dimension for a completely logical, closed universe is actually to violate another basic demand for rationality, since rationality has its moral, as well as intellectual, demands.

To achieve a satisfactory balance between the competing claims of the four dimensions of rationality is an important problem, we may infer, for the moral life of man. The process of settling the competing claims is described in a brilliant passage in *A Pluralistic Universe*.

But rationality has at least four dimensions, intellectual, aesthetical, moral, and practical; and to find a world rational to the maximal degree *in all these respects simultaneously* is no easy matter. Intellectually, the world of mechanical materialism is the most rational, for we subject its events to mathematical calculation. But the mechanical world is ugly, as arithmetic is ugly, and it is non-moral. Morally, the theistic world is rational enough, but full of intellectual frustrations. The practical world of affairs, in its turn, so supremely rational to the politician, the military man . . . is irrational to moral and artistic temperaments; so that whatever demand for rationality we find satisfied by a philosophic hypothesis, we are liable to find some other demand for rationality unsatisfied by the same hypothesis. The rationality we gain in one coin we thus pay for in another; and the problem accordingly seems at first sight to resolve itself into that of getting a conception which will yield the largest *balance* of perfect rationality of every description.[64]

James opposes here and in many other places, over and over again, the alleged right of other dimensions to veto the demands of morality. Thus, to those who would make of sensitiveness and refinement ideals which could legitimately ignore the demands of rigorous moral conduct, James points out the competing claims of morality. For example, he contrasts the devotion of Renan and Zola to sensibility *for its own sake* with the true but much-reviled view that conduct, and not sensibility, is the ultimate fact for our recognition. In doing so, James clearly implies, of course, that his sympathies are with him who stresses good conduct.

> No matter how we feel; if we are only faithful in the outward act and refuse to do wrong, the world will in so far be safe, and we quit of our debt toward it. Take, then, the yoke upon our shoulders; bend our neck under the heavy legality of its weight; regard something else than our feeling as our limit, our master, and our law, be willing to live and die in its service,—and, at a stroke, we have passed from the subjective into the objective philosophy. . . .[65]

Here, as he affirms the claims of morality, we should note that James conceives of the moral burden as a "heavy yoke." It is appropriate and necessary at this point for him to do so. If morality is only one of the several dimensions of rationality competing for our acceptance, then the rejection in any one instance of competing dimensions, with their many attractions, is bound to make the affirmation of the moral dimension less attractive and, perhaps, a real sacrifice. But, later, when we shall consider the knowledge imparted through mystical experiences, we shall see how mystical knowledge, throwing the whole business of rationality into radically new perspectives, makes the claims of other dimensions less attractive and makes the yoke of the moral life easy and joyful.

Meanwhile, in analyzing the moral implications of pragmatism, we must emphasize the fact that logical requirements do not play a major determining part in fulfilling the requirements of rationality. When the mind, for example, demands that ambiguity about the future be removed and that expectancy be defined, it is asking for more than logical consistency.

Thus, an ultimate datum which is such as to define expectancy, even though it be "logically unrationalized," will be "peacefully accepted by the mind." "Now in the ultimate explanations of the universe which the craving for rationality has elicited from the human mind, the demands of expectancy to be satisfied have always play a fundamental part."[66] Moreover, if several conceptions are "equally fit to satisfy the logical demand, that one which awakens the active impulses, or satisfies other aesthetic demands better than the other, will be accounted the more rational conception, and will deservedly prevail."[67] Viewed in terms of moral implications, this means that of two equally logical viewpoints on a moral problem that one which awakens and satisfies moral impulses is the more rational and the one to be one to be preferred by philosophy.

Furthermore, James declares as a basic principle that our *"passional nature"* not only *"lawfully may, but must, decide an option between propositions, whenever it is a genuine option that cannot by its nature be decided on intellectual grounds; for to say, under such circumstances, 'Do not decide, but leave the question open,' is itself a passional*

*decision,—just like deciding yes or no,—and is attended with
the same risk of losing the truth.*"[68] Continuing in the same
line, in *A Pluralistic Universe* he says that philosophy "is
more a matter of passionate vision than of logic, . . . logic
only finding reasons for the vision afterwards. . . ."[69] Philosophy and all of our knowledge are products not merely of the
intellect but also of the sensations and the emotions.

In examining James's views on knowledge, we may be
misled by the fact that his statements about rationality are
exclusively subjective as far as they are concerned with
criteria proposed for accepting a belief as rational. This
subjectivity we now propose to supplement and correct by
considering his views on the nature of truth and its connections with concrete reality.

For James, the problem of truth is one of the most basic
and central of all the problems of philosophy; ". . . the
establishment of the pragmatist theory of truth is a step of
first-rate importance in making radical empiricism prevail."[70] The real problem is not what is *the* truth, since "*the*
truth" is not an object of experience and therefore does not
exist.[71] The problem is rather to explore the nature of those
truths which exist as a plurality in our experience. What
are the characteristics of those experiences which we design-
ate by the name of *truth*?[72]

For a pragmatist, the importance of a truth lies in its
"practical" rather than in its theoretical significance;[73] a
truth is an instrument, a mental mode of adaptation to
reality, not primarily an answer to an enigma. A belief is
considered true if it accords with our other usual thoughts
and perceptions; if it conforms to reality, both abstract and
concrete; if it serves as a means of access to corresponding
objects.

Truth is not something already existing in the world,
awaiting discovery by the mind. Rather it is made, just as
health, wealth and strength are made, in the course of ex-

perience. "Truth . . . becomes a class-name for all sorts of definite working-values in experience."[74]

Against the rationalist view that truth itself is immutable, the pragmatist asserts that, since experience is "in mutation," truth, too, is subject to process, growth, and change. "Truths emerge from facts; but they dip forward into facts again and add to them; which facts again create or reveal new truth. . . . The 'facts' themselves meanwhile are beliefs that start and terminate among them."[75]

Against the rationalist theory that truth is largely a matter of *copying* reality, the pragmatist opposes the dynamic viewpoints that truth consists both in *a leading* to reality by means of ideas and in *a creation* of new realities by truth itself.

Even though James rejects the theory that truth is a matter of copying, he does make some statements such as the following: "An experience, perceptual or conceptual, *must* conform to reality in order to be true."[76] *"Our ideas must agree with realities,* be such realities concrete or abstract, be they facts or be they principles, under penalty of endless inconsistency and frustration."[77] How, then, should these be understood?

In neither of these quotations should conformity to reality or agreement with reality be viewed as meaning merely copying or reduplicating reality. Pragmatically, what purposes would be served by producing a second, and perhaps inferior, edition of reality? To conform or to agree means, rather, something dynamic, practical, and purposeful, the addition of something worthwhile to the world. Conforming and agreeing do not mean a static relationship, but rather refer to a *"satisfactory working* or *leading."*[78]

From the frequency of copying in the knowledge of phenomenal fact, copying has been supposed to be the essence of truth in the matters rational also. Geometry and logic, it has been supposed, must copy archetypal thoughts in the Creator. But in these abstract spheres there is no need of assuming archetypes. The mind is free to carve so many figures out of space, to make so many numerical collections, to frame so many classes and series, and it can analyze and compare so endlessly, that the very superabundance of the resulting ideas makes us doubt the 'objective' pre-existence of their models.[79]

(This question about the objective pre-existence of ideas is relevant, of course, to the problem of objective moral standards. We shall refer to it again near the end of this chapter, when we consider "back-door variations" of experience and the evidence for "necessary truths."[80] Indeed, not until then shall we be able to examine fairly the possibilities for the existence of an objective ethics within the framework of James's pragmatism; our present explication should be regarded as largely a preparation for that examination.)

To return to the problem of truth, we find that James considers only one truth "indefectibly certain," namely, "the truth that the present phenomenon of consciousness exists."[81] This is the only truth of which we can be certain. Even if we were to assume that it is a fact that truth exists and that our minds can find it, we could not know for sure, even when we had attained truth, that what we had was indeed the truth. "To *know* is one thing and to know for certain *that* we know is another."[82]

This empiricist way of believing in the truth, namely, that it exists, but that we cannot know for sure when we have it, follows from the contention that "truth cannot be a self-proclaiming set of laws, or an abstract 'moral reason,' but can only exist in act, or in the shape of an opinion held by some thinker really to be found." But, since no visible thinker is "invested with authority," shall we "simply proclaim our own ideals as the law-giving ones?"[83] Obviously, we should not. Therefore, we must admit that we cannot know for sure whether a given belief is true or not true.

However, setting aside this theoretical approach to the question (which cannot be settled), we find that, for practical purposes, there are sound pragmatic tests of the truth of concrete beliefs. *"True ideas are those that we can assimilate, validate, corroborate, and verify. False ideas are those that we cannot."*[84]

To be true, a belief must refer to something within "the framework of the pragmatic system";[85] all ideas, concepts, and scientific theories must "harmoniously lead back to the world of sense."[86] The true is "only the expedient in the way of our thinking,"[87] in the sense that it leads us to "beneficial interactions";[88] the "more 'true' " is the "more 'satisfactory' " as opposed to being, as intellectualists would have it, merely the more rigorously final.[89] "The chain of workings which an opinion sets up *is* the opinion's truth, falsehood, or irrelevancy, as the case may be."[90]

> To agree in the widest sense with reality can only mean to be guided either straight up to it or into its surroundings, or to be put into such working touch with it as to handle either it or something connected with it better than if we disagreed. Better either intellectually or practically. . . . Any idea that helps us to deal, whether practically or intellectually, with either the reality or its belongings, that doesn't entangle our progress in frustrations, that *fits* in facts, and adapts our life to the reality's whole setting will agree sufficiently to meet the requirement. It will be true of that reality.[91]

Briefly, then, the "essential thing" about a concrete truth is the "process of being guided";[92] "all that the pragmatic method implies is that truths should *have* practical consequences."[93]

Finally, the pragmatic method, stressing the value of the practical consequences of truth, allows us to believe that "the superiority of one of our formulas to another may not consist so much in its literal 'objectivity,' as in its congruity with our residual beliefs."[94] (Here we find the possibility, if all other courses should fail, of vindicating our moral beliefs on the grounds of their usefulness, their beauty, and their congruity with our other beliefs.)

As a result of the pragmatic account of truth, our mind has become "tolerant of symbol instead of reproduction, of approximation instead of exactness, of plasticity instead of rigor."[95] We see that truth means "the relation of less fixed parts of experience (predicates) to relatively more fixed parts (subjects) ; and we are not required to seek it in a relation of experience as such to anything beyond itself."[96] In knowing, we do not merely reproduce reality: "In our cognitive as well as in our active life we are creative."[97]

In exercising this creative role, man chooses to attend to certain limited aspects of reality to the exclusion of others. If he should, for example, choose to examine human behavior and do so solely from the viewpoint of its being a product of biological conditioning, he would be carving out of the great chaos of experience a perfectly legitimate area for study. His conclusions in such a study might be true, even though they portrayed man without his moral dimension. Another man, choosing another aspect of human behavior, might reach different conclusions, which, in turn, could be equally true.

The implication for morality here is that the moralist is free to reject positivistic or materialistic assertions that morality does not exist. The materialist errs when he thinks that moral phenomena do not exist. His mistake comes from believing that his approach to reality is the only correct one. But, as James clearly indicates, the way of the moralist is just as true in his own context as the way of other knowers in their own contexts.

The moralist has every bit as much right to stake out and describe an area of knowledge as has, for example, a physicist. The moralist's motivations in doing so, his methods (if he is a pragmatist) , and his findings are just as legitimate as those of any scientist. Although the area which he chooses for study is more subjective in nature than the areas chosen by some scientists, still it is just as capable of becoming a legitimate object of knowledge.

The manner in which truth is thus subject to the creative interests in man is summarized in Perry's *Thought and Character of William James* in the following illuminating analogies:

> While for other philosophers truth is a "discovery," for pragmatism it is an "invention." Like any technological device, it depends on the properties of nature, but is none the less a creation of the human mind. Or, to change the figure, truth is a "route" which man takes in traversing nature: the route must conform to nature, but so far as nature is concerned other routes might equally well have been discovered, laid out, and followed. When routes are once established they constitute those general characteristics of the human mind which make up common sense, or which philosophers call "the categories."[98]

"The desire," says James, "for a certain kind of truth here brings about that special truth's existence."[99] May we not infer, therefore, that if one should want to show that it is true that there are *no* moral truths, one could do so simply by carving out of experience particular aspects of reality in which one could indeed find reality without morality? The answer to this question is somewhat complex. First, as to James's statement, we must note that in its original context it definitely refers to "questions concerning personal relations, states of mind between one man and another."[100] It refers specifically to "truths dependent on our personal action."[101]

But what of general truths such as this one, namely, that there are (or are not) moral truths? To what extent, if any, are such general truths dependent upon our personal action? The answer is that they are indeed dependent upon personal action, but they rest not on the basis of intellectual decisions, but on decisions of the will:

> *Moral questions* immediately present themselves as questions whose solution cannot wait for sensible proof. A moral question is not of what sensibly exists, but of what is good, or would be good if it did exist. Science can tell us what exists; but to compare the *worths,* both of what exists and of what does not exist, we must consult not science, but what Pascal calls our heart. Science herself consults her heart when she lays it down that the infinite ascertainment of fact and correction of false beliefs are the supreme goods for man. Challenge the statement, and science can only repeat it oracularly, or else prove it by showing that such ascertainment and correction bring man all sorts of goods which man's heart in turn declares. *The question of having moral beliefs at all or not having them is decided by our will.* [Italics have been added.] Are our moral preferences true or false, or are they only odd biological phenomena, making things good or bad for us but in themselves indifferent? How can your pure intellect decide? If your heart does not *want* a world of moral reality, your head will assuredly never make you believe in one.[102]

While it may seem then that the truth of morality is, in a sense, "created" by us, we must understand that it is created, however, not in complete arbitrariness but in the general way in which the truths of the sciences are created by us. Moral truths, like the truths of the sciences, arise originally because of our personal desires and interests; in turn, these are confirmed by our will when it says that we shall believe in the existence of such truths and shall try to live in accord with them (or, in the case of science, when our will decides that the ascertainment of facts and correction of false beliefs are *the* goods for man) .

Thus, while we may not say that belief in moral truths is established on intellectual grounds, neither may we say that such belief is completely capricious. Rather, this belief is firmly grounded in man's real desires for a moral order; and, being thus established, such a belief is on a firm foundation for James—firmer than any intellectual foundation could possibly be for him.

Since knowing is only one of several possible ways for man to get into fruitful relations with reality,[103] knowledge, we infer, has no business in arrogating to itself the privilege of being the sole legitimate foundation of science and morality. The senses and emotions also have claims, and these claims must be respected when we construct a philosophy or a science.

Moreover, as James notes in other connections, man's subjective demands provide a more permanent basis for science and morality than do any of man's rational constructions. Theories come and go (e.g., the physics of Aristotle), but man's desires (e.g., his desire for a moral order) remain constant. Therefore, for James, the decision of the will motivated by man's desires constitutes a stable basis for a moral theory or a science; he regards this basis as superior to the intellectual basis provided by the rationalists.

Man, we repeat, engenders truth, is a partner in the production of truths, moral and otherwise.[104] This most important creative role of man is mentioned over and over by James. To illustrate the variety of ways in which he suggests this essential role, we submit the following typical passages:

In our cognitive as well as in our active life we are creative. We *add,* both to the subject and the predicate part of reality. . . . Man engenders truth upon it [the world].[105]

. . . reality is an accumulation of our own intellectual inventions.[106]

A priori, however, it is not self-evident that the sole business of our mind with realities should be to copy them.[107]

Why may not thought's mission be to increase and elevate, rather than simply to imitate and reduplicate existence?[108]

Truth we conceive to mean everywhere, not duplication, but addition; not the constructing of inner copies of already existing realities, but rather the collaborating with realities so as to bring about a clearer result.[109]

Although man's creative role in engendering truths introduces important subjective elements into knowledge, it does not follow that knowledge is an arbitrary production of man. As a feeling (or "idea"), an act of cognition involves self-transcendence: we "reserve the name knowledge for the cognition of 'realities,' meaning by realities things that exist independently of the feeling through which cognition occurs."[110]

For the feeling to be cognitive in the specific sense, then, it must be self-transcendent; and we must prevail on the gods to *create a reality outside of it* to correspond to its intrinsic quality q. Thus only can it be redeemed from the condition of being a solipsism. If now the new-created reality *resembles* the feeling's quality q, I say that the feeling may be held by us *to be cognizant of that reality*.[111]

Thus we say that for a feeling to be cognitive it must refer to a reality outside of itself. This implies, of course, that there *is* something outside the feeling, and that that something is a real thing. One may very well ask then what is our warrant for calling something *real*. James's answer is disarmingly simple: "The only reply is—the faith of the present critic or inquirer."

At every moment of his [the present inquirer's] life he finds himself subject to a belief in *some* realities, even though his realities of this year should prove to be his illusions of the

next. Whenever he finds that the feeling he is studying con-
templates what he himself regards as a reality, he must of
course admit the feeling to be truly cognitive. We are ourselves the critics here; and we shall find our burden much
lightened by being allowed to take reality in this relative
and provisional way. Every science must make some assumptions. *Erkenntnistheoretiker* are but fallible mortals. When
they study the function of cognition, they do so by means
of the same function in themselves. . . . *The most we can
claim is that what we say about cognition may be counted as
true as what we say about anything else.*[112]

(The two passages which we have just quoted are essential
to an understanding of the possibility of mystical experiences,
wherein the mystic believes he has knowledge of a transcendent, ineffable reality; they are essential also when we
wish to evaluate the feeling of self-transcendency in our
beliefs in certain necessary truths. As already mentioned,
mysticism and necessary truths will be discussed later in
some detail.)

In all this discussion of knowledge, however, we must
be careful not to lose sight of the fact that "theories" have to
forego the privileged status they occupied in "vicious" intellectualism. Theories are "at best a substitute for something
better, namely, first-hand observation—which is better both
as affording evidence of existence and as revealing its nature."[113] Theories were distasteful to James whenever they
were given the power of veto over the results of concrete
observations or were made to substitute for experience.
However, it is not correct to claim therefore, as Perry does,
that James demanded a philosophy which would exalt feeling and sensation above the intellect,[114] for intellectual
life is as concrete and pragmatic as is sense experience.

For James, sensation, the concrete, and the perceptual
flux were richer and "more real" than the abstract and all
static schemes of reality. If, therefore, logic finds itself at

odds with the perceptual flux, then so much the worse for logic. We must stick to the data of experience, both in the order of thought and in the order of sensation. But if we have to choose between "concepts inwardly absurd" and "the opaquely given data of perception," it is better to accept the data of perception.[115]

> The [perceptual] flux can never be superseded. We must carry it with us to the bitter end of our cognitive business, keeping it in the midst of the translation even when the latter proves illuminating, and falling back on it when the translation gives out. 'The insuperability of sensation' would be a short expression of my thesis.[116]

As we have seen, James insisted that we must respect all three departments of the mind, the thinking, the willing, and the perceiving. As a matter of fact, James heartily agreed with Locke's view on the *priority* and *preeminence* of particulars. He considered perception as affording a surer proof of existence because perception is *concrete* and *given,* "as distinguished from the abstract and mind-made generalizations of thought. This doctrine James drew together from various passages of the *Essay* (Locke's) , and labelled 'empiricism.' "[117] In *The Principles of Psychology,* James approved the doctrine that "though there be a great number of considerations wherein things may be compared one with another, and so a multitude of relations; yet they all *terminate in,* and are concerned about, those simple ideas either of sensation or reflection, which I think to be the whole materials of all our knowledge."[118] "Sensations are the stable rock, the *terminus a quo* and the *terminus ad quem* of thought. To find such is our aim with all our theories. . . . Only when you deduce a possible sensation for me from your theory, and give it to me when and where the theory requires, do I begin to be sure that your thought has anything to do with the truth."[119]

As a matter of fact, however, it is actually impossible, in the world in which we live, to "disentangle the contributions of intellect from those of sense."[120] "Pure sensations," James observes, *"can only be realized in the earliest days of life.* They are all but impossible to adults with memories and stores of associations acquired."[121]

Of importance for its moral implications is James's insistence, in *The Principles of Psychology,* that "sensations 'clustered together' cannot build up more intellectual states of mind."[122] He sees sensations, not as the building stones of higher mental functions, as do the sensationalists; rather, he insists that "sensations are immutable psychic things which coexist with higher mental functions."[123]

This doctrine in the *Psychology* might seem to imply that moral ideals, being higher intellectual states of mind, are independent entitities, not to be viewed as derived from or compounded of lower psychic activities. But in *A Pluralistic Universe,* and elsewhere, James considered the arguments for the doctrine that "higher" thoughts are not psychic units but compounds of "lower" thoughts. This we must keep in mind when we discuss, later on, his views on necessary truths, which are taken largely from the *Psychology.*

The suggestion that we should seek to attain perfect clearness in our thoughts of an object by considering the sensations, immediate or remote, we are to expect from it[124] contains a number of difficulties. Pure sensations, as we have seen, are practically impossible for adults. A further difficulty is revealed by James in *A Pluralistic Universe* (his last book) , when he examines the complications that develop when we actually confront a concrete reality.

> Take any concrete finite thing and try to hold it fast. You cannot, for so held, it proves not to be concrete at all, but an arbitrary extract or abstract which you have made from the remainder of empirical reality. The rest of things invades and overflows both it and you together, and defeats

your rash attempt. Any partial view whatever of the world tears the part out of its relations, leaves out some truth concerning it, is untrue of it, falsifies it. The full truth about anything involves more than that thing. In the end nothing less than the whole of everything can be the truth of anything at all.

Taken so far, and taken in the rough, Hegel is not only harmless, but accurate. There is a dialectic movement in things, if such it please you to call it, one that the whole constitution of life establishes; but it is one that can be described and accounted for in terms of the pluralistic vision of things far more naturally than in the monistic terms to which Hegel finally reduced it.[125]

Viewed thus, the application of the doctrine that concrete sensations are to be regarded as the touchstone of reality is far more complicated than one would first suspect it to be.

While it is true that perceptions, sensations, and the concrete all play very decisive roles in our knowledge, nevertheless it is necessary for human minds to operate on other levels also. For example, if we should wish to explain anything, we would find ourselves co-ordinating "one to one, the *thises* of the perceptual flow with the *whats* of the ideal manifold, whichever it be." This "theoretic conquest over the order in which nature orginally comes" takes place in conception.[126]

Conception, as well as sensation, is important in our study. To understand the implications of James's epistemology for his view on morality, we need an explication of the intimate, fruitful relationships between concepts and percepts. Just as our views on metaphysical problems, for example, can be distorted by a misuse of concepts, or a misunderstanding of the nature of concepts and their place in the total scheme of reality, so also can our views on moral questions be led astray. Therefore, an understanding of the nature of conception, a warning against its misuse, and a description of the fruitful, two-way traffic between conception and perception are essential to our study.

Conception, we are told, is a "means by which we handle facts by thinking them";[127] concepts are "ways of *handling* the perceptual flux and *meeting* distant parts of it; . . . [conception is] a faculty superadded to our barely perceptual consciousness for its use in practically adapting us to a larger environment than that of which brutes take account."[128] "Concepts are notes, views taken on reality, not pieces of it, as bricks are of houses";[129] they are ways of knowing things "representatively"[130] as opposed to knowing them immediately.

Although they are "only man-made extracts from the temporal flux,"[131] concepts are nevertheless "as real in the realm which they inhabit as the changing things in the realm of space."[132] Concepts are "realities of a new order";[133] "the non-perceptual experiences [i.e., concepts] have objectivity as well as subjectivity."[134]

The conceptualism here expressed by James affirms the objective reality of concepts and rejects the extremes of nominalism. While, on the one hand, stressing the priority of perception to conception, both genetically and cognitively, James's empiricism avoids, on the other hand, denying the reality of concepts.

James was fully aware of the discrepancy between concepts and reality in as much as the former are static and the latter is dynamic; however, he believed that the failure of conception is made good by perception, that "concepts are 'real' in their 'eternal way,' [that] they enter into close union with perception, and [that] they play an important role in experience. . . ."[135] Concepts and relations between them are just as *real* in their *eternal* way as percepts are in their temporal way.

For a pragmatist, a thing is real if it fits the following definition: "anything is real of which we find ourselves obliged to take account in any way."[136] It is obvious, therefore, in terms of this definition, that concepts are real: "Concepts are thus as real as percepts, for we cannot live a moment without taking account of them."[137] Therefore, we can conclude with James that his special treatment of conception combines "logical realism with an otherwise empiricist mode of thought."[138]

In accepting concepts as real, James is obliged by his own pragmatism to show that concepts perform useful functions. This they do, indeed, for concepts are teleological instruments. By taking up where percepts can carry us no further, concepts complement perceptual knowledge; percepts and concepts remedy one another's shortcomings.[139]

> We of course need a stable scheme of concepts, stably related with one another, to lay hold of our experiences and to co-ordinate them withal. . . . The immutability of such an abstract system is its great practical merit; the same identical terms and relations in it can always be recovered and referred to—change itself is just such an unalterable concept . . . they [i.e., abstract concepts] *have no value but these practical values.*[140]

These practical values of concepts are of great importance for life and philosophy, and especially for morality.[141] Concepts "bring new values into our perceptual life, they reanimate our wills";[142] concepts provide us with standards and perspectives.

That our concepts pass the pragmatic test is due in no small part, we may infer, to the fact that conceptual knowledge is required for moral values. Without concepts we could not have a single rule of conduct or a single moral ideal. As James notes, "life's values deepen when we translate percepts into ideas! The translation appears as far more than the original's equivalent."[143] For example, when we "translate" our perception of a heroic act into its conceptual equivalent, we transform and enrich our perception. The concept of heroism complements the thickness of the perception with a luminousness and depth peculiar to conception.

On the other hand, once we are equipped with concepts, we find that we have guides to steer us through the labyrinth of life with its confusing mazes of sensations. As useful teleological instruments, concepts help us to survive and prosper in this world. Moreover, by means of concepts, we are able to make a re-evaluation of life, a task certainly of great importance for our moral development.[144]

We are able to use concepts in guiding ourselves through life and in evaluating our actions and perceptions only because there is a most intimate and active traffic between percepts and concepts, as they mutually influence and guide one another.

> The whole universe of concrete objects, as we know them, swims . . . for all of us, in a wider and higher universe of abstract ideas, that lend it its significance.[145]

> With concepts we go in quest of the absent, meet the remote, actively turn this way or that, bend our experience, and make it tell us whither it is bound.[146]

> An experience is "understood" when it is referred to some place in the conceptual realm.[147]

> If what we care most about be the synoptic treatment of phenomena, the vision of the far and the gathering of the scattered like, we must follow the conceptual method.[148]

> But what we thus immediately experience or concretely divine is very limited in duration, whereas abstractly we are able to conceive eternities.[149]

However, despite their great services to mankind, concepts have grave limitations as pictures of reality, and the misuse of concepts by rationalists and absolutists has caused much havoc in philosophy.

Among the various limitations of concepts, perhaps the gravest is their inability to represent change. "Whatever actual novelty the future may contain (and the singularity and individuality of each moment makes it novel) escapes conceptual treatment altogether. Properly speaking, concepts are post-mortem preparations, sufficient only for retrospective understanding. . . ."[150] As a result, a man who uses concepts to foresee new situations must always do so only "in ready-made and ancient terms."[151]

Philosophers, therefore, who regard concepts, with their eternally unchanging contents, as superior to perceptions distort both thought and the perceptual flux. Far from being superior to percepts, "conceptual knowledge is forever inadequate to the fulness of the reality to be known."[152] *"Am anfang war die tat;* the fact is a first; to which all our conceptual handling comes as an inadequate second, never its full equivalent."[153]

Vitally important as they are, concepts can be (and are) misused. To prevent their misuse, James makes the following points:

> Thought deals . . . solely with surfaces. It can name the thickness of reality, but it cannot fathom it, and its insufficiency here is essential and permanent, not temporary . . . it is . . . static and schematic and lacks . . . many of the characters which temporal reality possesses.[154]

> They [concepts] make the whole notion of a causal influence between finite things incomprehensible. No real activities and indeed no real connexions of any kind can obtain if we follow the conceptual logic. . . .[155]

> Instead of being interpreters of reality, concepts negate the inwardness of reality altogether.[156]

> . . . it [intellectualism] makes experience less instead of more intelligible.[157]

In view of these limitations of conceptual knowledge, we can follow James's meaning quite easily when he assails the so-called absolute superiority of our higher thought: "all that it can find is impossibility in tasks which sense-experience so easily performs."[158]

Concepts, so valuable when properly employed, become a menace to philosophy when their functions are perverted by intellectualism. As used by vicious intellectualists, concepts are "clung to even when they make things unintelligible."[159]

It is a fatal intellectual error to make static concepts the sole source of knowledge; to do so, is to find ourselves "inveterately wedded to the conceptual decomposition of life."[160] This decomposition, in which we reduce reality to essences and knowledge to definitions of essences, is given philosophic respectability by the vicious intellectualists. Against this unwarranted acceptance of such a distortion of thought James made ceaseless warfare. He particularly opposed what he called the viciousness of intellectualism which comes, he said, from "the habit of employing them [i.e., concepts] privatively as well as positively, using them not merely to assign properties to things, but to deny the very properties with which the things sensibly present themselves."[161] "The treating of a name as excluding from the fact named what the name's definition fails positively to include, is . . . 'vicious intellectualism.' "[162]

Because of the limited perfections of concepts, James rejects all claims made for the superiority of conceptual systems such as mathematics, logic, aesthetics, and ethics. The alleged superiority of such systems, resting on the exclusion of the facts of the perceptual flux, must be rejected. True superiority lies in perception because "perceptual reality involves and contains all these ideal systems, and vastly more besides."[163] Moreover, all conceptual systems are viewed as imperfect in the sense that their one necessary characteristic, namely, simplicity, is a most inadequate equivalent for the highly complex world which they represent: "a simple conception is an equivalent for the world only so far as the world is simple,—the world meanwhile, whatever simplicity it may harbor, being also a mightily complex affair."[164]

We infer, therefore, that ethical conceptions are a poor equivalent of the rich data of perceptual knowledge and moral phenomena. We cannot, for example, learn about the moral life merely by referring to ethical systems. The concepts which constitute such systems "are not *parts* of reality, not real positions taken by it, but *suppositions* rather, notes taken by ourselves, and you can no more dip up the substance of reality with them than you can dip up water with a net, however finely meshed."[165]

When they deal with *moral facts,* concepts are even more unsuccessful than when they deal with external things. While things that lie in the world of space, things of the sort that we literally *handle,* are what our intellects cope with most successfully, we know "the inner movements of our spirit only perceptually. We feel them live in us, but can give no distinct account of their elements, nor definitely predict their future. . . ."[166]

> But the sciences in which the conceptual order chiefly celebrates its triumphs are those of space and matter, where the transformations of external things are dealt with. To deal with moral facts conceptually, we have first to transform them, substitute brain-diagrams or physical metaphors, treat our ideas as atoms, interests as mechanical forces, our conscious "selves" as "streams," and the like.[167]

We can expect, then, that the difficulties of a moralist in creating an adequate system of ethics will be greater than the difficulties of a scientist in creating, let us say, a science of chemistry. In addition to the grave problems which he shares with all who attempt to translate the perceptual flux into conceptual systems, the moralist also has special problems associated with the translation of moral facts into concepts, facts which do not lie in the world of space.

However, once the translation has been made and the conceptual system set up, both the chemist and the moralist find that they have concepts which are eternally true, independent of the world of sense, and valid only in so far as they can be put to practical uses.

The so-called eternal truth of such conceptual systems is a result of the process of abstraction, which drops out all notions of change. Actually, such immutability in concepts is a perfection only because it is a useful quality for the knower; it is a gross imperfection in so far as it involves a distortion of the constantly changing character of reality.

Once we have created a conceptual system, it will be found to possess an independent existence. "It suffices all by itself for purposes of study. The 'eternal' truths it contains would have to be acknowledged even were the world of sense annihilated."[168]

The test of the "map" provided by conceptual system and of the "eternal truths" which it contains is made by seeing how effectively they help us to handle our experiences. The essential office of concepts is to "coalesce with percepts again, bringing the mind back into the perceptual world with a better command of the situation there";[169] "particular consequences are the only criterion of a concept's meaning, and the only test of its truth."[170]

> It is possible therefore, to join the rationalists in allowing conceptual knowledge to be self-sufficing, while at the same time one joins the empiricists in maintaining that the full *value* of such knowledge is got only by combining it with perceptual reality again. This mediating attitude is that which this book must adopt.[171]

If we were to grant that self-sufficing systems of ethics, containing "eternal truths," may exist, such systems would have value only by their applications to perceptual reality, not in their "beauty" or "sublimity" as independent spiritual realities "untainted" by the perceptual flux. On the other hand, the given order of the perceptual flux with its masses of moral data is "a chaos of experience,"[172] and requires remodelling if it is to have any meaning for us. Fortunately, this order of experience lends itself to remodelling and "shows itself plastic to many of our scientific, to many of our aesthetic, to many of our practical purposes and ends."[173]

Thus, perception and conception interpenetrate and co-operate in the production and application of ethical systems. The world of ethical propositions, having been abstracted and generalized from long-forgotten perceptual instances from which it has, as it were, flowered out, returns and merges itself again "in the particulars of our present and future perceptions."[174] For ethics, just as for other fields of knowledge, we need both percepts and concepts; neither, taken alone, knows reality in its completeness. But, on the other hand, in ethics and other conceptual systems, wherever there arises a conflict between the evidence of perception and of conception, our Radical Empiricism leads us to accept the evidence of perception and reject the concept.[175] "Use concepts when they help," James advises, "and drop them when they hinder understanding; and take reality bodily and integrally up into philosophy in exactly the perceptual shape in which it came."[176]

We can see now that pragmatism, in its "positivistic tough-mindedness," does not scorn every rationalistic notion so long as it is valid, but attempts really to find a place in the scheme of philosophy for conceptual knowledge. Pragmatism does not love "intellectual anarchy as such," nor does it prefer "a sort of wolf-world absolutely unpent and wild and without a master or a collar."[177] Rather it defends the use of conceptual knowledge—but does so only so far as it redirects us fruitfully into experience.

However, against the dogmatic assertion that rationalism is the *only true* philosophy because it alone satisfies intellectual demands, James declares that the satisfaction of intellectual demands is *only one* of the requirements for an acceptable philosophy. "The interest of theoretic rationality, the relief of identification, is but one of a thousand human purposes. When others rear their heads, it must pack its little bundle and retire till its turn recurs."[178] James insisted that the rationalist himself was governed by "passion" even as he chose his own rationalistic philosophy; he declared that subjective elements could and should contribute to philosophy.

Taking such a typically rationalistic demand as that which calls for consistency at all costs, James declares that this is not, as rationalists declare it to be, a purely intellectual demand. Speaking of this demand as an "appetite," James says that it is "nothing but the *passion* for conceiving the universe in the most labor-saving way. . . ." Moreover, if this so-called law of parsimony is made the exclusive law of the mind, it "will end by blighting the development of the intellect itself quite as much as that of the feelings or the will."[179] Its demands for acceptance on the grounds that its credentials are purely intellectual and coercively infallible is, of course, unacceptable in terms of pragmatism and Radical Empiricism.

As a matter of fact, not only do we find "our passional nature influencing us in our opinions," but, more than that, "there are some options between opinions in which this influence must be regarded both as an inevitable and as a lawful determinant of our choice."[180] Some such options refer to questions which play vital roles in moral life, for example, the option between belief in free will and determinism, an option which must be determined finally on the basis of our passional nature.

Thus our emotions do, and should, play a part in the formation of knowledge. The rationalist's rejection of the emotions is absurd. For example, when the absolutist insists that complete detachment is the only acceptable attitude in an investigation, he is pragmatically wrong. We can see that the man who has no interest whatsoever in the results is bound to be incapable. "The most useful investigator, because the most sensitive observer, is always he whose eager interest in one side of the question is balanced by an equally keen nervousness lest he become deceived."[181]

The rationalist belief that theory is superior to emotions is denied by James because experience shows that "in some men theory is a passion, just as music is in others."[182] Such men pursue the form of inner consistency "beyond the line at which collateral profit stops."[183] Thus, the basic rationalist belief that only conceptual knowledge is true knowledge is just one of many such beliefs which men hold because the belief itself satisfies a subjective craving in the individual.

As a matter of experience and observation, we know that the knowledge which we possess is not, and cannot be, purely intellectual. "Pretend what we may, the whole man within us is at work when we form our philosophical opinions. Intellect, will, taste, and passion co-operate just as they do in practical affairs. . . ."[184] "Evidently, then, our non-intellectual nature does influence our convictions. There are passional tendencies and volitions which run before and others which come after belief."[185] Such passional influences do not invalidate the knowledge which they shape.

One reason why the emotions may legitimately play a part in the shaping of our knowledge is that the emotions, too, are themselves characterized by *extradition*. Just as knowledge is characterized by the self-transcendency of its object, so also emotions point to an object as the cause of the present feeling. "What is called 'extradition' is quite as characteristic of our emotions as of our senses."[186]

> What an intensely objective reference lies in fear! In like manner an enraptured man and a dreary-feeling man are not simply aware of their subjective states; if they were, the force of their feelings would all evaporate. Both believe there is outward cause why they should feel as they do: either "It is a glad world! how good life is!" or "What a loathsome tedium is existence!"[187]

As we have already seen, our emotional and practical subjectivity sets the ends for which the conceiving or theoretical department of the mind functions. But apart from this extremely important role, the emotions have other characteristics which also call for our attention. These characteristics are vividly described in *The Varieties of Religious Experience,* as follows:

> Individuality is founded in feeling; and the recesses of feeling, the darker, blinder strata of character, are the only places in the world in which we catch real fact in the making, and directly perceive how events happen, and how work is actually done. Compared with this world of living individualized feelings, the world of generalized objects which the intellect contemplates is without solidity or life.[188]

By presenting feeling as a kind of cognition and by assigning to it an important part in the perception of spiritual facts, James has prepared the way for us to appreciate the importance of feeling in his ethics. The importance and validity of the parts played in our knowledge by the emotions are further shown by the indispensable role which they perform in all scientific knowledge. Although many partisans

of science deny that the emotions—regarded by them as subjective, inferior kinds of experience—play any part at all
in scientific knowledge, their very ardor on behalf of scientific method itself betrays its own non-intellectual origins.
On closer inspection, the so-called impersonal viewpoints of
scientists and of the partisans of sciences are disclosed to be
not nearly so impersonal or unemotional as they are said
to be.

Far from having an "independent" existence, science itself
proves to be a human construction, created by men largely
in order to satisfy their craving for a more rational and
coherent account of their experiences. "The popular notion
that 'science' is forced on the mind *ab extra,* and that our
interests have nothing to do with its constructions, is utterly
absurd. The *craving to believe* that the things of the world
belong to kinds which are related by inward rationality
together [*sic*], *is the parent of Science* as well as of senti-
mental philosophy. . . ."[189]

Far from suggesting that the moralist or the philosopher
should adopt the alleged impersonality of the scientist's
approach, James actually disparages several claims made on
behalf of science. Speaking of the much admired "impersonal" view of science, he says that it may one day appear
to have been only a "temporarily useful eccentricity."[190]
Speaking of the scientific method, he declares that science
has made the mistake of falling so deeply in love with the
method that she "has ceased to care for truth by itself at
all."[191] Speaking about the "philosophy" of evolution, which
was enjoying such prestige in his day, James affirms that it
is "a metaphysical creed," "a mood of contemplation, an
emotional attitude,"[192] rather than a system of thought.
Finally, he declares that scientists are the most insufficient
authorities as to the total nature of reality: their interests,
he says, "are most incomplete and their professional con-
ceits and bigotry immense."[193] "I know of no narrower sect

or club, in spite of their excellent authority in the lines of fact they have explored. . . . Their only authority *at large* is for *method*—and the pragmatic method completes and enlarges them there."[194]

Far from presenting a picture of the perceptual flux as it really is, the order of scientific thought actually is "quite incongruent either with the way in which it really exists or with the way it comes before us."[195] In science we "break the solid plenitude of facts into separate essences, conceive generally what only exists particularly, and by our classifications separate the contiguous and join what the poles divorce."[196] Regarding their faithfulness to reality, the best we can say for our scientific systems is only that some of the relations among the objects of our scientific thought are *"congruent* with the time-and-space relations which our impressions affect."[197]

This inability of science to make a complete and accurate representation of all reality is, however, not necessarily regrettable. As a matter of fact, certain essential attributes of reality, being intrinsically mysterious, call for responses which cannot be made by science. The "wonderfulness" and "mysteriousness"[198] which reality does display call frequently for us to react by other means. Instead of cognition, the appropriate human action at this point is the "emotion of ontological wonder."[199] Instead of being angry because we cannot wrest all the secrets from reality, we should be grateful that we can approach things at all. "Data! gifts! something to be thankful for! It is a gift that we can approach things at all, and, by means of the time and space of which our minds and they partake, alter our actions so as to meet them."[200]

Science, which men generally regard as the most perfect expression of truths accessible to man, is itself limited by the opaqueness of reality, by the limited applicability of the scientific method, and by the imperfections of man as a knowing being. What, we may ask, does that mean for the whole problem of truth? Where, specifically, does it leave us with that problem with reference to the problem of certitude?

That this problem of certitude is an important one James never doubts. Our answers to the questions of certitude bear directly on one of man's central concerns, namely, his wish to be right. This concern James affirms to be *the one interest* of concrete man. "That [i.e., to be right] for him is the art of all arts, and all means are fair which help him to it."[201] For us, in our special concern about the moral implications of James's pragmatism, this problem is important, and James's answer is crucial to the basic matter of the truth of moral standards.

His own answer to the problem of certitude is forced on James by his Radical Empiricism. Since *all* experience is a constantly changing process, he must say that "no point of view can ever be the last one."[202] Any opinion which we currently hold is, therefore, subject to modification by subsequent experiences, and opinions must never be regarded as absolutely certain.[203]

As a matter of fact, in addition to this *theoretical* difficulty, there are also concrete, *practical* problems about the possibility of having absolutely certain knowledge. No one has ever devised a test of what is really true and at the same time been able to get universal agreement as to the validity of that test. Some have made the criterion of truth external to the moment of perception, and others have made the perceptive moment its own test. But, no matter what they have set up as criteria, "the much lauded objective evidence is never triumphantly there." In the last analysis, "one's conviction that the evidence one goes by is of the real objective brand, is only one more subjective opinion added to the lot."[204]

But the fact that these difficulties exist does not mean that we must give up the quest for truth. While declaring himself to be a complete empiricist so far as his theory of human knowledge goes, James nevertheless says that giving up the doctrine of objective certitude does not mean also giving up "the quest or hope of truth itself."[205] "We still pin our faith," he declares, "on its existence, and still believe that we gain an even better position towards it by systematically continuing to roll up experiences and think."[206]

This giving up of the doctrine of objective certitude will have to be related to James's views on the existence of necessary truths, a matter of basic importance for ethical standards. This we shall attempt to do as soon as we have discussed some necessary preliminaries, namely his views on the role of hypotheses and faith in the formation of knowledge.

Although we are obliged to deny the *doctrine* of objective certitude, we are, fortunately, still able to find and use concrete truths, truths which can pass pragmatic tests in specific situations in life. In the formulation of these truths, we find that both hypothesis and faith play important parts.

Against the notion that science should admit only demonstrated truths, James declares that every science "must make some assumptions."[207] He asserts that the living facts of human nature show that "every philosopher, or man of science either, whose initiative counts for anything in the evolution of thought, has taken his stand on a sort of dumb conviction that the truth must lie in one direction rather than another, and a sort of preliminary assurance that his notion can be made to work; and has borne his best fruit in trying to make it work. . . ."[208]

Insofar as hypotheses serve useful functions, the philosopher should admit them. "On pragmatic principles we can not reject any hypothesis if consequences useful to life flow from it."[209] Such hypotheses may be accepted no matter where they originated; rationalistic claims about the sovereignty of the intellect are to be ignored. "It matters not to an empiricist from what quarter a hypothesis may come to him: he may have acquired it by fair means or by foul; passion may have whispered or accident suggested it. . . ."[210] If a hypothesis is a *live* one, a man takes a chance no matter what he decides; even if he refuses to make a positive or negative decision he still has cast a vote thereby for a certain attitude towards the hypothesis.

> And when an hypothesis *is* once a live one, one risks something in one's practical relations towards truth and error, whichever of the three positions (affirmation, doubt, or negation) one may take up towards it. *The individual himself is the only rightful chooser of his risk.*[211]

After adopting a hypothesis, the empiricist watches to see how it fits in with the rest of experience; "if the total drift of thinking continues to confirm it, that is what he means by its being true."[212] Herein the methods of the sciences, proceeding by hypothesis and verification, are the ideal for the individual in his concrete judgments and for philosophy itself.

> Since philosophers are only men thinking about things in the most comprehensive possible way, they can use any method whatsoever freely. Philosophy must, in any case, complete the sciences, and must incorporate their methods. One cannot see why, if such a policy should appear advisable, *philosophy might not end by forswearing all dogmatism whatever, and become as hypothetical in her manner as the most empirical science of them all.*[213]

As an empirical science, philosophy will be expected to follow the scientific method and be satisfied with the relatively modest claims of science, which when properly advanced make no claim to dogmatic certitude. Philosophy will start always with hypotheses and will subject them in the course of experience to a process of verification. Philosophical truths, accordingly, will be regarded as true in exactly the same way in which scientific truths, properly regarded, are true—in other words, philosophy, like science, will provide us with concepts that will help us to get into fruitful connections with reality. Thus all philosophical truths, including the truths of ethics, will be based upon hypotheses and subject constantly to verification by experience.

We see that philosophy, including ethics, is, like science, a human construction. Into it enter, quite legitimately, man's hopes and aspirations; even more so than logic the actions and emotions of man establish the basis and framework of philosophy. Philosophy, as a human construction, comes from many aspects of man.

Important among the subjective contributions in the making of knowledge is an element which James frankly and simply calls *faith*. Against the cautious, fearful attitude which causes men to postpone beliefs until all the desired evidence is in, he urges us to put faith in our cravings and in the possibilities of arriving at concrete truths without waiting for conclusive intellectual proofs.

Faith in the favorable outcome of a search for truth is not any more culpably emotional and subjective than, let us say, fear of making an error. While we agree that truth should be our goal, it does not necessarily follow that fear of error is more sound philosophically than hope for success. "Dupery for dupery, what proof is there that dupery through hope is so much worse than dupery through fear?"[214]

Therefore, since our attitude towards the possibility of finding a concrete truth is bound to involve some emotion on our part, we may as well favor that particular emotion, if there is such a one, that makes more possible the formulation of the truths. There is such an emotion, and it is simple faith.

As a matter of fact, although we may adopt an attitude lacking in faith when we confront some options for belief, we find that, regarding the general possibility of knowledge, faith is forced upon us, whether we wish it or not. "The coil is about us," says James, "struggle as we may. The only escape from faith is mental nullity."[215] He adds, "We cannot live or think at all without some degree of faith. Faith is synonymous with working hypothesis."[216]

The man who rejects faith on the grounds that the emotions should not be allowed to enter into the formulation of truth finds himself in a strangely inconsistent position. He claims to reject the role of faith because such a role introduces inconsistent elements into his allegedly consistent intellectual scheme of knowledge. But, at the same time, his own preference for consistency, asserted at any price, is itself a subjective craving just as much as is faith. "Intellectualism's proclamation that our good-will, our 'will to believe,' is a pure disturber of truth is itself an act of faith of the most arbitrary kind."[217]

Since our faculties of belief were given us to live by, we actually are *forced* into doubting, believing, and denying. We are forced to take positions towards possibilities, by affirming, doubting, or denying them, even where verification is incomplete. In all cases where we face a situation wherein alternatives are practically and vitally important to us, this compulsion makes neutrality inwardly difficult and outwardly unrealizable. The intellectualist's position is theoretically and practically untenable. (In moral conduct, we therefore infer, we must act decisively in some cases even where objective evidence regarding the theory or the facts is inconclusive.)

Faith is not merely an inescapable element of cognition; its role in knowledge is truly valuable and creative. As we have seen, no matter what attitude a man adopts with reference to knowledge, his action necessarily involves faith to some degree (at least faith in his own knowing processes, or faith in his own doubts about them) . In addition, as we shall see, faith is not to be viewed as an undesirable impurity in cognition; rather it is "in fact the same moral quality which we call courage in practical affairs. . . ."[218] Faith, whereby we assume a risk in the cause of knowledge, is analogous to courage, whereby we assume a risk on behalf of some other interest of ours.

Faith, as described by James, is a many-sided reality. His main ideas can be summarized by saying that faith is: (1) a presupposition which is necessarily involved in every mental act (belief, doubt, etc.) ; (2) a readiness to act on behalf of causes regarding whose success we may still have some doubt; (3) in certain classes of truths, an ingredient making for the realization of the object believed in; (4) the best possible response to a need to accept personal responsibility in forming opinions on the larger questions of life (a response which is best described genetically in the process called the "faith-ladder," a "slope of good-will on which in the larger question of life men habitually live") ;[219] (5) an expression of life which exceeds logic; (6) "the practical reason for which the theoretic reason finds arguments after the conclusion is once there."[220]

Point (4) is, of course, most important in terms of its moral implications. On the most important questions of life, especially moral questions and questions with moral relevance, men find themselves *forced* to turn to faith. To refrain from decision or action merely because of the failure of the intellect to provide conclusive answers to moral questions would be to fail in one's duty as a human person; the only alternative in the absence of "conclusive knowledge" is courageously to embrace, in an act of faith, that belief which satisfies our cravings. Since, as a matter of fact, the intellect often does fail to answer moral questions of practical and theoretical importance, the right to believe must be recognized and exercised. Experience has shown that acting on our faith is often prophetic and right, and James praises, for example, our willingness to run the risk of acting on the basis of our "passional need of taking the world religiously."[221]

The process whereby we formulate our beliefs on the larger questions of life is, as we have said, the so-called faith-ladder. After we have somehow obtained a particular conception of the world or of conduct, we ask ourselves if it is true or not, and, in some cases, we arrive at a belief in it by going through the following process, called the faith-ladder:

> It *might* be true somehow, you say, for it is not self-contradictory. It *may* be true, you continue, even here and now. It is *fit* to be true, it would be *well if it were* true, it *ought* to be true, you presently feel. It *must* be true, something persuasive in you whispers next; and then—as a final result—It shall be *held for true*, you decide; it *shall be,* as if true, for *you.*[222]

Affirming the truth of a belief on the basis of "mere" faith is, according to James, a natural right of the individual if such affirmation answers to the needs of the man. Faced as a man is with the necessity of living his life in the short span that he has, he cannot indefinitely postpone vitally necessary decisions and actions. What should he do, then, in such cases, in the absence of intellectually verified criteria for thoughts and actions? Obviously, he should, and must, go ahead and act on the basis of the only means available to him—on the basis of his desires and his faith. Whatever a man does here, whether he doubts or believes, he is making a personal decision and he acts on his own responsibility and risk.[223] To do so is indeed his right—no matter what the intellectualists may say to the contrary.

For the moralist, faith, taken as a factor making for the realization of the object believed in,[224] has special significance. We may, for example, in our relationships with a man whose moral attitudes towards us are bad, behave in several ways. We may choose to follow our own cravings for a good world and better human relationships; in doing so, we choose also to believe that our enemy is capable of being morally good, and we further believe he may well change his attitude towards us for the better. As a matter of fact, experience shows that this kind of belief often is an important factor in bringing about a desirable moral change; it shows, too, that affirmation of the contrary moral belief on our part may influence our enemy's moral character for the worse. No matter what we choose to believe, in instances of this type, however, our faith is an important factor, actually or potentially, in bringing about a moral change in ourselves and others. This role of faith is important and legitimate.

In view of this phenomenon, whereby *"faith in a fact can help create the fact,"*[225] it would be absurd to accept the intellectualist's insistence that we should *not* let faith run ahead of "scientific evidence." To restrict our beliefs within the limits proposed by scientific absolutists actually would decrease our moral effectiveness in the world immeasurably. So to decrease the successes of moral influences would be, obviously, a tragic mistake.

But to say that we should believe in, and act on, those opinions which best satisfy our cravings requires considerable clarification from the moral point of view. If we ask whether James means that we are acting morally when we affirm whatever we wish merely because it gratifies our selfish desires, we must seek an answer in pragmatism as James sees it.

An opinion is true, we recall, just as an action is good—when it is "expedient," that is, when it helps us to cope successfully with our concrete problems. Which actions or opinions will help us most we can discover by examining our experiences and seeing how they actually work out. If experience shows that brutal, selfish actions, for example, are truly the most "expedient," then these would be indeed moral actions. But, as a matter of fact, we may infer from the general tenor of his teachings, James believes that experience definitely proves that selfish and brutal actions do not truly contribute to a better life for us; and, despite whatever apparent advantage selfishness and brutality seem to offer, they are really against life and are indeed immoral.

To understand the moral "expediency" of a given act, it must be seen in the largest possible context of human experiences. Ideally, this context should include not only all experiences in the visible world but also relationships with the invisible order. It must be seen in the world envisioned by Radical Empiricism, a world freed from the static universe of vicious intellectualism. Thus seen, ethics is freed from those kinds of logics and legalisms which reflect only the static order of a frozen, intellectualistic world.

While corrosive subjective elements can be introduced into ethics by pragmatism through its use of the word "expedient," James's interpretation of the word provides, in his own case, a picture of concrete goods which still resembles the presentation of great traditional moralists on the same subjects (for example, the subjects of justice, love, and kindness). While there is the possibility of interpreting pragmatism not only as James interpreted it, but also, for example, as Mussolini did, this possibility does not necessarily condemn James's use of pragmatism. It is, of course, clear that pragmatism means different things to each of those men, but this is because the basic moral commitment involved in determining whether an action is expedient or not is different in each case.

Since the pragmatic method itself can be judged by its fruits, we may apply the pragmatic test to the ethics which is derived pragmatically. What, therefore, do these radically different conclusions of James and of Mussolini imply? They actually mean that the pragmatic method depends upon the metaphysical context in which it is applied and the meaning given to the word "useful." Given James's Radical Empiricism and his notion of "useful" with reference to the moral life, and given also his devotion to his search for the truth, his pragmatism leads him to unselfish defense of morality and profound reverence before the phenomena of saintliness in which moral life reaches its highest perfection. "Let us be saints, then, if we can, whether or not we succeed visibly."[226] "The saint is therefore abstractly a higher type of man. . . ."[227]

In this connection we can see how essential Radical Empiricism is for James's ethics. Without it, his pragmatism would be, at best, ethically ambiguous. In telling us that we should judge an act entirely by its *results* and not by its doctrinary basis it would be fatally incomplete; it would leave the individual without an objective criterion for evaluating "results." Which, then, we could ask, is the morally desirable result, Mussolini's powerful state erected at the expense of the individual, or James's democratic republic?[228] There is, however, a way out of this ambiguity; it lies in the radical acceptance of all experiences and, especially, in the acceptance of "necessary truths."

In the Radical Empiricism in which James works out his pragmatism, we shall see the possibility of having objective standards which grow up in our experience. (There we see how James finds objective standards which will, for example, condemn Mussolini's tyranny and sanction James's humanism. These objective standards appear with the experiencing of what James calls "necessary truths." The objective standards are grounded in such truths.)

In *The Will to Believe*, James declares that man has "inexpugnably" established himself "in the necessary."[229] Man is led to the necessary by trusting his wants and following the uneasiness which they occasion; thus he is led to issues entirely beyond his present powers of reckoning.

Using the empirical approach, that is, examining experience in order to discover what is real, James, in *The Principles of Psychology,* discovers evidence that there are some "necessary truths," possessing characteristics which all other kinds of truths lack. The data one obtains by thus examining one's mind may be summarized as follows: (1) Some natural experiences (*e.g.,* aesthetic ones) seldom come up to our expectations (*e.g.,* our "aesthetic demands") . (Does this not mean that some things, *e.g.,* the principles of aesthetics, are independent of "experience"?) (2) Certain ideas have intrinsic necessity. The nature of the ideas of blueness and of yellowness allows us to compare them but forbids us to try to infer one from the other or make one a genus for the other. Experience cannot overthrow this necessity. (3) Systematic classification and logic are results of the capacity for discerning difference and likeness: this capacity has nothing to do with the order of experience. (4) Likewise, pure sciences form a body of propositions with whose genesis experience has nothing to do. (5) The abstract scheme of successive predication constitutes an immutable system of truth, flowing from the very form and structure of our thinking. (6) The axiom of skipped intermediaries is not a purely formal law of thinking, but flows from the nature of the matters thought about. (7) *In some cases, instead of experience engendering "inner relations," inner relations are what engender the experience.*[230]

Now, two basic doctrines of Radical Empiricism are implicated in these data, namely, the doctrine that all reality is experiential (or that no trans-empirical reality exists) and the doctrine that all experience is undergoing constant change. If there are such things as necessary truths (any analysis of mental experiences indicates that there are), then they must exist as experiences, and yet they must somehow be free from the changing character of all other experiences. How can this be explained?

When we examine our higher aesthetic, moral, and intellectual life, we find concepts which cannot be explained genetically by experience, as we have generally used that term. If this be true, then we must either deny the truth of such concepts (since they lack experiential validation) or modify the meaning of the word experience. James, in *The Principles of Psychology*, preserves our higher aesthetic, moral, and intellectual life by modifying the meaning of experience. He does this by distinguishing two types of experience.

In *The Principles of Psychology*, James says that the word *experience* refers to two distinct ways in which the mind is "assailed," although the word's use is generally restricted to mean only one of those ways. The first type, the way of *experience* in the usual sense of the word, is the "front-door" way; here, knowledge enters through the five senses, and the agents which affect the brain in this way immediately become the mind's objects.[231] The second type of experience is the "back-door" way; here, knowledge originates "inside" the person, and the agents produce perceptions which take cognizance of something other than the agents.

In the case of front-door experiences, the agents are natural objects (like sunsets, etc.) , which impress the brain "through the senses, and in the strict sense of the word give it *experience*, teaching it by habit and association what is the order of . . . [its] ways."[232] But the agents of back-door experiences are in the brain itself or elsewhere in the body, being natural objects or processes "which equally modify the brain, but mould it to no cognition of *themselves*."[233]

The pure, or *a priori*, sciences of classification, logic, and mathematics, and our higher aesthetic, moral, and intellectual life are made up of these back-door or "house-born" experiences: "the pure sciences form a body of propositions with whose genesis experience has nothing to do."[234]

While the pure sciences and our higher aesthetic, moral,

and intellectual life are made up of back-door experiences which are not derived from "experience" as James usually uses the term, the natural sciences seem to come from a combination of both types of experiences. They involve front-door experiences which are subjected to a thorough reorganization and translation in terms of experiences which were "house-born." James describes the order of thought in the natural sciences in the following passage. We quote it here because we might infer that somewhat the same process would take place if one were to organize a kind of Jamesian applied ethics.

> The order of scientific thought is quite incongruent either with the way in which reality exists or with the way in which it comes before us. Scientific thought goes by selection and emphasis exclusively. We break the solid plenitude of fact into separate essences, conceive generally what only exists particularly, and by our classifications leave nothing in its natural neighborhood. . . . What we experience, what *comes before us,* is a chaos of fragmentary impressions interrupting each other; what we *think* is an abstract system of hypothetical data and laws.[235]

Now we see that the crude order of experience is transformed in science by concepts which arise from a special kind of experience. As a matter of fact, we "invincibly crave" to alter the given order of nature as it is given us by front-door experiences because we find that there are other relations among things which are "more charming." "These other relations are all secondary and brain-born, 'spontaneous variations' most of them, of our sensibility. . . ."[236] Such house-born experiences, having a real inward fitness, impel us to reorganize the crude data of front-door experience in a more satisfactory way.

The fact that such a reorganization takes place in the form of ideals which are not to be found among front-door experiences proves, for James, that the ideals themselves must not come through the senses. *"These are then,"* he says, *"ideal and inward relations amongst the objects of our thought which can in no intelligible sense whatever be interpreted as reproductions of the order of outward experience."*[237]

The non-sensory origin of ideals is further demonstrated by the very fact that such ideals and the testimony of the senses are often in conflict with one another. In the aesthetic and ethical realms, for example, the house-born experiences conflict with the order of the front-door experiences. As James points out, "the early Christian with his kingdom of heaven" tells the world "that the existing order must perish, root and branch, ere the true order can come."[238] (But the objects of "scientific" thought do not conflict with the order of front-door experiences, being *"congruent with the time-and-space-relations which our impressions affect."*) [239]

At this point we now see that there are such things as back-door experiences which are morally relevant. As we have just seen, James thinks of these back-door moral experiences as conflicting often with corresponding experiences which have originated through the senses; this conflict, inseparable from ethics, can never be resolved. Therefore, ethics may never establish, as the natural sciences do, any absolute congruence between its back-door and front-door types of experience.

What does this imply with reference to the possibility of a "system" of ethics based upon pragmatism and Radical Empiricism? From the following quotation we may infer that James thinks such a system is possible: "In other words, though nature's materials lend themselves slowly and discouragingly to our translation of them into ethical forms, but more readily into aesthetic forms; to translation into scientific forms they lend themselves with relative ease and completeness. The translation, it is true, will probably never be ended."[240]

If a system of ethical conceptions is possible, it will, of course, share many of the characteristics of other types of conceptual systems. It will pay us, therefore, to examine briefly those characteristics.

The possibility of having conceptual systems, in James's philosophy, rests upon James's decision to restrict his nominalism to things in the perceptual flux and to eliminate it with reference to concepts.[241] Concepts he conceives as real beings, and, therefore, scientific knowledge is viewed as a real possibility.

Such scientific knowledge is both useful and valuable, even though the conceptualization of the perceptual flux always involves some falsifications. The damage done by conceptualization, however, should be kept to a minimum, and the fact that conceptualization *does* involve falsifications must always be borne in mind. As thinkers, we must "take account of a reality by *preserving* it in as unmodified a form as possible . . . we must preserve all the experience we can and minimize contradiction in what we preserve. . . ."[242]

In the construction of a conceptual system (such as ethics), the theorizing faculty of the mind "transforms the world of our impressions into a totally different world,—the world of our conception. . . ."[243] This transformation is a man-made product; in the case of the *"a priori* sciences" (for example, logic and mathematics), there is no immediate connection at all with fact. The eternality of the properties and relations of triangles, squares, genera, etc., is due to the fact that they are only improvised human artifacts, which we have *decided* to make invariant. The relations remain invariant because we have *made* the objects invariant.[244] But in the case of conceptual systems other than the *a priori* sciences, the necessity of the concepts must be explained in some other way.

This necessary nature in the case of such conceptual systems cannot be explained away as being merely the result of habit or of the experiences of the race. In aesthetics, for instance, the necessary character of aesthetic principles cannot be entirely explained as a result of habit, even though the principle of habit will explain the connections to some extent. As James says, "When a conjunction is repeatedly experienced, the cohesion of its terms grows grateful [sic], or at least their disruption grows unpleasant. But to explain all aesthetic judgments in this way would be absurd; for it is notorious how seldom natural experiences come up to our aesthetic demands."[245] In ethics, also, the necessary character of our principles cannot be explained altogether by "habitual experiences having bred inner cohesions. Rightness is not mere usualness, wrongness mere oddity, however numerous the facts which might be invoked to prove such identity."[246]

Neither can we say that the necessary character of moral judgments is simply the result of the pressures exerted upon us by public opinion. "The most characteristic and peculiarly moral judgments that a man is ever called on to make are in unprecedented cases and lonely emergencies, where no popular rhetorical maxims can avail, and the hidden oracle alone can speak; and it speaks often in favor of conduct quite unusual and suicidal as far as gaining popular approbation goes."[247]

We see, too, that the necessary character of scientific concepts cannot be explained by the theories of the apriorists or by the theories of the evolutionary empiricists. There is no evidence at all for the theory of the apriorists that such necessity is explained by the organic structure of the mind or any other transempirical reality; neither is there satisfactory evidence for the evolutionary theory that the necessary character of concepts arises from the experiences of man's ancestors. The only satisfactory explanation, says James, is that the necessary character of a concept arises as a "spontaneous variation" among the back-door variety of experiences.

Such experiences do arise only because man's "whole life . . . [is] a quest for the superfluous"; if it were not such a quest, he "would never have established himself so inexpungably as he has done in the necessary."[248] In his "discovery" of the necessary, his wants, and the uneasiness which they occasion, set him on the road of discovery; the discovery itself comes to us in the form of "lucky fancies," and "it is only *apres coup* that we find that they correspond to some reality."

> Our abstract and general discoveries usually come to us as lucky fancies; and it is only *apres coup* that we find that they correspond to some reality. What immediately produced them were previous thoughts, with which, and with the brain-processes of which, that reality had naught to do. Why may it not have been so of the original elements of consciousness, sensation, time, space, resemblance, difference, and other relations? Why may they not come into being by the back-door method, by such physical processes as lie more in the sphere of morphological accident, of inward summation of effects, than in that of the 'sensible presence' of objects? Why may they not, in short, be pure *idiosyncrasies,* spontaneous variations, fitted by good luck (those of them which have survived) to take cognizance of objects (that is, to steer us in our active dealings with them), without being in any intelligible sense immediate derivatives from them? I think we shall find this view gain more and more plausibility as we proceed.[249]

Arising thus as "spontaneous variations," our scientific concepts are fitted to take cognizance of objects and to steer us in our dealings with them. Our moral principles, "house-born" as they are, must also be seen as having meaningful references to realities existing in the perceptual flux. In this respect, however, ethics (and aesthetics) differs from the physical sciences in the manner in which its principles are related to the data in the perceptual flux. This relationship in ethics does not display the same kind of congruence which we find between scientific laws and corresponding physical phenomena. We know, as a matter of fact, that in the case of ethics there is commonly a conflict between the data of the front-door experiences and the house-born principles, which, as we have seen, is absent in matured physical sciences, or, at least, is a sign of imperfection if it exists in the conceptions of such sciences. In ethics such a conflict is not necessarily a sign of imperfection in our conceptual system.

Our study of the ethical implications of James's pragmatism, with reference specifically to his views on knowledge, has shown that James's pragmatic epistemology definitely does provide a basis for ethical concepts, or, better still, it has shown that his epistemology is founded on his ethics.

As they stand, those ethical views which are explicitly or implicitly contained in James's Radical Empiricism and pragmatism are fairly definite, and James often expounds them with ardor and passion. The fact that he never provided them with a systematic exposition should not blind us to the importance which James assigned to moral questions. For him, morality was a central problem for the philosopher.

Of the views on ethical questions expressed by James, we shall, for the conclusion of this chapter, present those which describe his general attitude towards the question of ethics as a branch of knowledge. In regard to that subject we may draw the following conclusions:

a) Ethics admits no *a priori* or transempirical basis; that is to say, it is entirely experiential.

b) Ethics is, however, not merely a description of man's actual concrete behavior.

c) Ethics provides "objective" standards of conduct, all of which grow up endogenously *within* the experiences of man.

d) Ethics accepts as true those concepts which are both (1) house-born and (2) "verified" *pragmatically* by front-door experiences as being concepts which help us successfully to cope with our practical, concrete problems.

e) Ethics is frankly based on our *will to believe* those concepts which answer our cravings for a moral order and direct us fruitfully in our dealings with our experiences; this point is based on pragmatic considerations.

f) Ethics rejects all intellectualistic demands that ethics be based on reasoning only. The "subjective elements," emotions and will, must be consulted and respected in constructing an ethics.

g) Ethics rejects all positivistic, evolutionary, and crude associational explanations of the genesis of the inner necessity of moral concepts. Against such explanations, James affirms the reality of the inner necessity of moral concepts.

h) Ethics denies that any one individual or group of men may rightfully have the final word on ethical questions.

i) Ethics is viewed as being expanded and corrected as men accumulate and absorb more and more experiences.

j) Ethics indicates on many concrete moral questions that *for pragmatic reasons* as well as for theoretical reasons one cannot say for sure what is the right answer. In such cases, mutual toleration of differences is pragmatically and theoretically the appropriate action.

k) Finally, pragmatic ethics insists, as we might expect, that all ethical propositions be submitted to practical tests: no ethical ideal is to be accepted unless it makes a useful contribution to man's mundane struggles in this life.

V

The Moral Life of Man

In our study we have, so far, examined the moral implications of pragmatism with special reference to James's views in metaphysics, religion, and epistemology. In every case morality was found to occupy a central position in his thought. Indeed, as we have observed, James believes that the problems of metaphysics, religion, and epistemology can be formulated and settled successfully only by keeping in mind their relevance to morality. The philosopher must, James says, in all cases, respect the claims of moral experiences. Thus, any religious, metaphysical, or epistemological viewpoints which would hamper the unfolding of man's moral life must be considered false viewpoints.

Having seen that James carefully develops his metaphysics, religion, and epistemology with scrupulous respect for the claims of moral experiences, we may now inquire regarding some positive points of his ethical philosophy. We shall develop several of these points and indicate their relationship to his pragmatism.

The central position which is occupied by the moral problem in James's philosophy has an analogue in the "resolute moral energy" which James views as being the "essential root" of the human personality. The value of this resolute moral energy is such that it extorts from us a respect that is not diminished even when we find it in persons who are inarticulate or unequipped with learning. Its value is further shown by the fact that, in the absence of such moral energy, the acutest theories, the greatest intellectual power, and the most elaborate education are a "sheer mockery." Indeed, when "mean motives" and a nerveless will, rather than a resolute moral energy, are the roots of intellectual achievements, we sense a great discrepancy between the facts of that case and the ideal situation wherein such achievements are fed by moral sources.[1]

Just as this resolute moral energy is the root of human personality so also the element of "seriousness" in the universe is one of the most important aspects of the world. Pragmatically speaking, we must affirm that this element of seriousness exists because its existence is indispensable to man: in order to live successfully, man must live morally; and to live morally he must have a universe which he can, must, and will take seriously. Therefore, we must conclude that ours is a universe of "a drastic kind . . . from which the element of 'seriousness' is not to be expelled."[2] The man who accepts a universe of this kind is, says James, a "genuine pragmatist."[3]

The true pragmatist is unalterably convinced, by pragmatic reasons, of the essentially moral nature of the universe. Indeed, he will accept and live on a scheme of possibilities which he holds to on trust, provided only that these possibilities provide fruitful connections between this radically moral universe and his own radically moral nature. In terms of this universe and of his own nature, he will frame ideals; and to realize these, he is willing, if need be, to pay even to the extent of sacrificing his own person.[4]

These ideals which the pragmatist frames are not regarded as existing *ante rem* as necessary principles, but are really seen as only a possible *terminus ad quem*.[5] His system of ideals is not "found" by the pragmatist, but is constructed through the selection and organization of such ideals as will best contribute to man's well-being; such ideals are pragmatically verified in terms of man's own experiences, not in terms of any transempirical or intellectualistic criteria. The ideal order of the world is, for the pragmatist, something which is an ultimate, not an origin, an extract, not the whole;[6] it is constructed, not to mirror some *a priori* order, but in order to create conditions favorable to the survival of the thinker.

Although the ideals of the pragmatist are, in a sense, created by the individual, they are, nevertheless, regarded also as not being merely arbitrary constructions. The pragmatist, as a matter of fact, demands, on the one hand, that his ideals have outward applications, and, on the other hand, he insists that outward reality must have moral characteristics which call for definite personal responses and forbid other responses. He rejects subjectivistic arbitrariness in all its forms and the contention that what happens in the universe is "subsidiary to what we think or feel about it."[7] For example, he denies the subjectivist's justification of crime, rejecting the argument that crime is justified because it awakens "our intelligence of that criminality"[8] and thus stimulates remorse and regret.

Proceeding empirically and respecting the data of experience, the pragmatist finds that experience leads him to believe in a certain objectivity in morality (that is, *objective* in the sense of being grounded in experience). This belief, in turn, forbids him to pretend to be neutral in moral questions: "Now it would contradict the very spirit of life to say that our minds must be indifferent and neutral in questions like that of the world's salvation. Any one who pretends to be neutral writes himself down as a fool and a sham."[9]

The objectivity thus attributed to morality must not, of course, be understood as implying in any way any "abstract

moral 'nature of things' existing antecedently to the concrete thinkers themselves with their ideals."[10] Ideals have
no existence until they are realized in the lives of those
thinkers who bring them into existence in order to deal
more effectively with their own concrete problems.

But once these ideals have been realized by concrete
thinkers, the ideals themselves are objectively real. Thus,
the pragmatist can, and must, approach the problems of life
with great moral earnestness, intent upon regarding life as
"a real fight, in which something is eternally gained for
the universe by success."[11] Indeed, pragmatism, having led
the philosopher to believe in a "radically moral universe,"
has made of him an "absolute moralist." And, as an absolute
moralist, the pragmatist must take his stand with moral
ideals, regardless of the disastrous consequences which might
follow for him.

> The absolute moralist, on the other hand, when his interests
> clash with the world, is not free to gain harmony by sacri-
> ficing the ideal interests. According to him, these latter
> should be as they are and not otherwise. Resistance then,
> poverty, martyrdom if need be, tragedy in a word,—such
> are the solemn feasts of his inward faith.[12]

The pragmatist thus takes his unselfish stand on behalf
of morality, even though he knows that no concrete moral
opinion, including indeed the one for which he may be
called on to die, can be regarded as final and absolutely
true.[13] Other men faced with similar uncertainty about ideals
might choose to avoid sacrifices which could turn out to
have been for unworthy ideals. *But in the absence of certain
proof even,* the pragmatist must act on behalf of his moral
ideals. As a matter of fact, as James says, countless men find
that the disseminated and strung-along successes which attend many moral acts are really sufficient to satisfy man's

rational needs. This satisfaction is, of course, adequate pragmatic justification for pragmatists to believe in and act on
on behalf of their moral ideals, even in the absence of
certainty.

The satisfaction we get out of good conduct is immeasurably increased if each success is viewed as "one moment in
the world's salvation."[14] Acting in concert with other men
of good will and with the finite deity who is their co-worker,
the pragmatist sees his deeds acquiring deeper significance
as they contribute to the shaping of this melioristic world.
Understanding that ideals are not self-sufficient, he knows
that they must be actualized, and he understands that ideals
ought to aim at *the transformation of reality*—no less!"[15]

The ethical maxims of such a pragmatist are not the
maxims of an impressionist, a romanticist, or a "partisan of
merely worldly efficiency."[16] Royce declares that the pragmatist's maxims win their way through "to a resolute interpretation of human life as an opportunity to cooperate with
the superhuman and the divine."[17] Similar views are expressed by Perry: "For James life assumes a heroic form only
when the moral subject believes in the superiority of his
own ideal, not merely as his, but as in some sense absolute
or infinite."[18]

Regarding the specific nature of those moral ideals which
play such an important role in life we may paraphrase and
quote James's observations in the following manner:

   a) Objective moral ideals involve the recognition of
"limits, foreign and opaque to our understanding."[19]

   b) Our moral responsibility ends with the performance of
our duty, "and the burden of the rest we may lay on higher
powers."[20]

   c) A moral act, when reduced to its simplest and most
elementary form, "*Consists in the effort of attention by
which we hold fast to an idea,* which but for that effort of
attention would be driven out of the mind by the other

psychological tendencies that are there. *To think,* in short, is the secret of will, just as it is the secret of memory."[21]

d) Over all these individual opinions about moral questions, the philosopher believes there is "a *system of truth* which he can discover if he only takes sufficient pains."[22]

e) The imperative character of a moral obligation exists in the concrete claim itself; it does not come from any abstract, inorganic imperativeness existing outside of the concrete claim.[23]

f) Conduct, not sensibility, is "the ultimate fact for our recognition." "No matter how we succeed in doing these outward duties, whether gladly and spontaneously, or heavily and unwillingly, do them we somehow must; for leaving them undone is perdition."[24]

g) "The question of having moral beliefs at all or not having them is decided by our will." "If your heart does not *want* a world of moral reality, your head will assuredly never make you believe in one."[25]

h) "The moral principles which our mental structure engenders are quite as little explicable *in toto* by habitual experiences having bred inner cohesions. Rightness is not *mere* usualness, wrongness not *mere* oddity. . . ."[26]

i) "The feeling of the inward dignity of certain spiritual attitudes . . . and of the essential vulgarity of others . . . is quite inexplicable except by an innate preference of the more ideal attitude for its own pure sake."[27]

j) Whether God exists or not, ethical ideals are nevertheless real; "ethics have as genuine and real a foothold in a universe where the highest consciousness is human. . . . 'The religion of humanity' affords a basis for ethics as well as theism does."[28]

k) "The various ideals have no common character apart from the fact that they are ideals."[29]

Moral ideals, then, being objectively real and vitally significant to man, call upon us for specific responses in terms of conduct. In forming our lives in response to the values, we are involved in an extremely complex process including, among others, psychological, sociological, and religious factors. To study that process, we should have to examine the role of the community and the individual in establishing moral standards, the psychological process of moral happiness, casuistry, the role of the emotions, the significance of ascetic practices, the differences between Christian and pagan goodness, the phenomenon of mysticism, and last, but by no means least, that pinnacle of goodness, saintliness.

For James, the moral judgments which we are called upon to make on the basis of our own unique personal confrontation with moral problems are more characteristically and peculiarly moral judgments than those which are made for us by the community. This James believes, even though he also admits the important contributions made by history and tradition in forming our standards of behavior. While he takes cognizance of the "layers" of human perfection which, for example, separate us from the Africans who pursued Stanley with cries of "meat, meat!"[30] still he feels that the really significant moral judgments made by the individual are *not* those that are "most invariably and emphatically impressed on us by public opinion." "The most characteristic and peculiarly moral judgments that a man is ever called on to make are in unprecedented cases and lonely emergencies. . . ."[31]

On the other hand, James points out that for the moral contributions of the individual to survive, the sympathy of the community is required. While the community will stagnate without the "impulse of the individual," that impulse itself will die if it does not receive a favorable response from the group.[32] Moreover, the importance of the community with reference to moral development can be verified simply by looking at history, where nothing is more striking than "the secular alteration that goes on in the moral and religious tone of men, as their insight into nature and their social arrangements progressively develop."[33]

For James, however, the greater interest is in the moral contributions, not of the community but of the individual. Since life is *"what we make it, from the moral point of view,"*[34] the individual has in each case the opportunity of making his life a moral success within the framework given to him. As the individual thus seeks to make his own life a moral success, we see further evidence of the importance of respecting individuality; James tells us that there can *not* be any *one* "intrinsically ideal type of human character."[35]

Not only is there no one type of human character which is ideal for all men, but also, we see, there is not a specific ideal type of response which is good under all circumstances for any one individual. Not only do individuals differ from one another but also a given individual at various times faces different moral situations and is called upon to make different kinds of responses. The moral element in human nature, therefore, does not mean any single quality; it means rather a group of qualities, out of which various specific qualities should be actualized on different occasions.

The pragmatic element in this viewpoint is evident in that no particular moral quality is valued for itself or held to be necessarily the best response for all occasions. As a matter of fact, that moral quality in any given situation is best which helps the individual to survive and get into fruitful relationships with reality.

The fact that no specific moral quality serves always as the best response to concrete situations does not mean, however, that there can be no unity in the moral personality of a man. Such unity is attainable, and, as a matter of fact, its attainment through the process of the development of character is one of our main goals in life. Indeed, the potentialities of such development in the souls of men are, according to

James, so great as to be "unfathomable."[36] This development takes place through various formative influences, some being directly subject to man's will and others being either indirectly or not at all subject to the will.

The formative influences which we find to be subject to our wills include voluntary attention and our beliefs. "Our acts of voluntary attention," says James, "brief and fitful as they are, are nevertheless momentous and critical, determining us, as they do, to higher or lower destinies."[37] Some beliefs, for example, the belief in the existence of a moral order, are at once subject to the will (the "will to believe") and at the same time indispensable for the development of character. Some beliefs are such that they must be affirmed before we can even enter the moral realm at all, and thus are affirmed for soundly pragmatic reasons.[38] Other beliefs which are also relevant to morality and directly related to character formation include those in which the sentiment of reality polarizes our whole life "through and through."[39] A belief in God, for example, will polarize all of our moral life and cause a reorganization of our character.

If we examine the moral life of various persons, we shall discover different types of character. The causes of such diversity lie chiefly in "our differing susceptibility of emotional excitement, and in the different impulses and inhibitions which these bring in their train."[40] Crystallized in the form of habits, these susceptibilities, impulses, and inhibitions bear us "irresistibly towards our destiny, whatever the latter may be."[41]

The differences of character, moreover, are such that some men can achieve certain qualities only through resolute voluntary action, whereas other men are born with those very qualities. Such qualities, says James, are at their best in men who have them as gifts of nature. "Your mere aspirant to a certain type of character . . ." he writes, "only shows, when your natural lover, fighter, or reformer, with whom the passion is a gift of nature, comes along, the hopeless inferiority of voluntary to involuntary action."[42]

Given a certain character, a man will find that its very uniqueness makes it impossible for him successfully to apply to his moral difficulties exactly the same solutions which have worked for other men. "Each, from his peculiar angle of observation, takes in a certain sphere of fact and trouble, which each must deal with in a unique manner."[43] Because every character is different, one man will have to soften himself and another man harden himself, while one man should yield a point and "another must stand firm."[44] One thing, regardless of these differences of character, is true of the moral life of all men, that is, the fact that "the normal evolution of character does chiefly consist in the straightening out and unifying of the inner self."[45] As long as a man's life is full of disorder, slackness, and vague superfluity, we can hardly even speak of him as having character at all. The process of inner moral unification, which corrects this disorder, may come in any number of ways: it may come gradually or abruptly, through altered feelings or altered powers of action, through new intellectual insights or through mystical experiences; this remedying of inner discord and incompleteness may take place with "any sort of mental material,"[46] religious or otherwise.

As we have seen, the process of inner unification may take place in any number of ways; when, however, an alteration does take place which is such that it involves the growth of any one aim to a point where it is so stable as to expel other aims definitively from the individual's life, we have an instance of a "transformation." These transformations can take place in such a way that we have sudden and complete conversions; "often amid tremendous emotional excitement or perturbation of the senses, a complete division is established in the twinkling of an eye between the old life and the new."[47] On the other hand, transformations of character may also take place gradually through the accumulation of small changes in thoughts, actions, and emotions.

The best thing that could happen in such transformation is for it to occur in such a way as to bring about a man's salvation, for in his salvation lies "the greatest of all facts *for him.* . . ."[48] Achieved through "accumulated acts of thought,"[49] rather than through maxims, salvation is a result of conduct rather than theories.[50]

The way to salvation that we infer from reading James is one that satisfies the demands of both empirical and pragmatic criteria. The virtues, for example, which man should acquire are found only in experience and are tested by pragmatic means. They have no reference to transempirical realities and have no value apart from their concrete usefulness to men. In discussing purity, for example, James affirms that *usefulness* is *the* basic element in determining the value of that virtue: "Purity . . . is *not* the one thing needful; and it is better that a life should contract many a dirt-mark, than forfeit its usefulness in its effort to remain spotless."[51]

The empirical and pragmatic aspects of James's theory about the nature of virtue are well presented in the following description of the virtue of prudence:

Suppose, e.g., that we say a man is prudent. Concretely, that means that he takes out insurance, hedges in betting, looks before he leaps. Do such acts constitute the prudence? Are they the man qua prudent? Or is the prudence something by itself and independent of them? As a constant habit in him, a permanent tone of character, it is convenient to call him prudent in abstraction from any one of his acts, prudent in general and without specification, and to say the acts follow from the pre-existing prudence. These are the peculiarities in his psycho-physical system that make him act prudently; and there are tendencies to association in our thoughts that prompt some of them to make for truth and others for error. But would the man be prudent in the absence of each and all of the acts? Or would the thoughts be true if they had no associative or impulsive tendencies? Surely we have no right to oppose static essences in this way to the moving processes in which they are embedded.[52]

Thus embedded as they are in the moving processes of life, the virtues by which we attain salvation have no existence and no usefulness apart from human experiences. The consideration which we show for virtues is not motivated by our recognition of any independent, *a priori* dignity which virtues are said to have apart from their concrete usefulness. We respect virtues only by reason of their concrete usefulness to us as we face life's problems.

Having no dignity *per se,* apart from their usefulness, virtues cannot be arranged in a hierarchy according to their intrinsic nobility. But the need to arrange the virtues in some kind of order of relative importance must be faced, nevertheless, because of a very practical need. As James says, ". . . the ethical philosopher's demand for the right scale of subordination in ideals is *the fruit of an altogether practical need.* Some parts of the ideal must be butchered, and he needs to know which part. It is a tragic situation, and *no mere speculative conundrum,* with which he has to deal."[53]

The philosopher's quest for the right scale of subordination in ideals, James observes, must be viewed as a mission which is indispensable to the moral life. Without some sort of casuistic scale "which keeps his more imperative goods on top," no man can enjoy perfect peace.[54] To attain this casuistic scale with any degree of success, a man must be guided by the following basic ideas:

That act must be the best act . . . which makes for *best whole,* in the sense of awakening the least sum of dissatisfactions. In the casuistic scale, therefore, those ideals must be written highest which *prevail at the least cost,* or by whose realization the least possible number of other ideals are destroyed.[55]

. . . the [casuistic] question always is—not a question of this good or that good simply taken, but of the two total universes with which these goods respectively begin.[56]

There is but one unconditional commandment, which is that we should seek incessantly, with fear and trembling, so to vote and to act as to bring about the very largest total universe which we can see.[57]

He [the moral philosopher] knows that he must vote always for the richer universe, for the good which seems most organizable, most fit to enter into complex combinations, most apt to be a member of a more inclusive whole.[58]

The task of solving the casuistic problem, fortunately, has been made much easier for the moral philosopher because much valuable work has been done already. As a matter of fact, a casuistic scale has been made by society, a scale which, through countless ages, has evolved through trial and error, and innumerable human experiments. The laws and usages of the land constitute such a scale, since they are what "yield the maximum of satisfaction to the thinkers taken all together."[59] To these pragmatically tested laws and usages the philosopher must turn when he is constructing his own casuistic scale, and, giving credit to conventionally recognized goods, he must "put the things most in accordance with the customs of the community on the top."[60] "The presumption in cases of conflict must be in favor of the conventionally recognized good."[61]

Opposed to this point of view, however, is James's belief that the most important and most significant moral decisions which a man is ever called upon to make are those which he must make by himself, apart from the group, and, often, in opposition to the group. Both of these viewpoints, different as they are, do, however, fit squarely within the pragmatic

criteria which James establishes for valid casuistic scales. We
know that the view favored by the group is morally valid
if it brings a desired good into actuality with a minimum
sacrifice of other goods—in other words, if it brings the
richest possible moral universe into being. On the other
hand, the solitary decision of the individual, dissenter
though he may be, is likewise valid if it fulfills the same kind
of conditions. No "closet-solutions" of philosophers can ever
tell *a priori* what sort of conduct will achieve the maximum
amount of goodness in this world. "These moral experiments
are to be judged, not *a priori,* but by actually finding, after
the fact of their making, how much more outcry or how
much appeasement comes about."[62]

From these experiential and pragmatic characteristics of
moral judgments it follows that no moral judgment can be
regarded as absolutely final. The philosopher can only hope
that, by following the "line of least resistance," he will
move towards the "richer and more inclusive arrangement."[63] Thus, if a particular kind of conduct in a given case
was found to make a richer and more inclusive moral universe, that conduct was right and good—but only for that
case. In any other instance we could not say for sure, in
advance of seeing the actual outcome, whether that same
conduct would be useful or not in achieving maximum goodness. In this respect, ethics is "just like physical science"; as
far as the casuistic question is concerned, ethics, "instead of
being deducible all at once from abstract principles, must
simply bide its time, and be ready to revise its conclusions
from day to day."[64]

The struggle to find a truly satisfactory casuistic scale, a
more and more inclusive moral order, is indeed the very
history of mankind. To invent some manner of realizing his
own ideals, while at the same time not denying other alien
demands, is the goal of man from generation to generation.
The goal which man seeks, James declares, requires a stable

and systematic moral universe; this universe is "fully possible only in a world where there is a divine thinker with all-enveloping demands. If such a thinker existed, his way of subordinating the demands to one another would be the finally valid casuistic scale."[65] The casuistic scale which man needs so desperately requires the existence of a divine being; needing such a being for the satisfaction of his own concrete needs and cravings, man, we infer, has every right to believe in such a being.

In addition to the problem of finding a scale to guide our conduct, a further problem remains to be solved, however, namely that of finding means whereby we can reorganize our moral lives so that they will conform to that scale. If such a scale existed but was allowed to remain only a theoretical concept, it would have no pragmatic significance at all. Lacking such significance, it would have no place in philosophy. Therefore, we see that the means whereby we change our characters in order to realize the most perfect moral order is vitally important; fortunately, men, through generations and generations, have worked out techniques and beliefs which improve the possibility of self-perfection. Historically, such techniques and beliefs reached their highest development in connection with various religions, Christian and non-Christian.

In all cases, successful techniques have always included ascetic practices as an essential part of moral self-improvement. At times these techniques were combined with beliefs that expressed a naturalistic self-sufficiency, and at other times with a belief in self-surrender, self-sufficiency characterizing the Stoic outlook and self-surrender the Jewish and Christian. Thus, to understand the two outlooks, James suggests that we compare Marcus Aurelius' "fine sentence: 'If the gods care not for me or my children, here is a reason for it,' with Job's cry: 'Though he slay me, yet will I trust in him.' "[66] A world of difference separates the Stoic's resignation from Job's self-surrender.

The views of the Stoics and Epicureans mark, James believes, a "certain definite stage accomplished in the evolution of the world-sick soul. They mark the conclusion of what we call the once-born period, and represent the highest flights of what twice-born religion would call the purely natural man."[67] The views of these highest expressions of pagan ethics, as compared with the views of those whose religion is non-naturalistic, are not characterized by joyousness, as one might expect, but by cheerlessness and unmitigated pessimism.[68] Where the resignation of the pagan brings at best cheerlessness, the self-surrender of Christians brings joy.

Between the spirit of Stoicism and the spirit of Christianity, both frankly and truly interested in morality, we discern undeniable gaps. Where the Stoic agrees *to* the scheme of the universe, the true Christian literally *abounds in agreement,* running out "to embrace the divine decrees."[69] Where the *animus mundi* of the Stoic is to be respected and submitted to, the Christian God is to be loved; where the Stoic accepts the universe in a drab discolored way, resigning to necessity, the Christian saints embrace the universe with "passionate happiness."[70] Even at his very best, the Stoic lacks something which the Christian saint has in abundant measure, something which makes of the Christian "a human being of an altogether different denomination."[71]

The resignation and the moral ideals which characterized paganism at its very best are rejected by the "twice-born" religions and replaced by behavior and beliefs which, seeking no happiness for the believer, do, most paradoxically, bring him a wealth of happiness, far exceeding any happiness ever achieved by pagans.

Since the true end of pragmatic philosophy is behavior,

the morality and the religious creeds which thus bring such an abundance of happiness are, of course, of profound interest to the pragmatist.[72] By its fruits, not by its roots, says the pragmatist, is a belief to be judged. If the morality and the creeds of Christian, Mohammedan, Hindu, and Buddhist saints bring those men peace and happiness, while all other kinds of conduct and theories fail miserably, then, regardless of their origins, their religions are shown by their fruits to be true with respect to the most significant matters in life. Twice-born religions appear, then, to have the successful answers to life's profoundest and most vitally significant riddles, regardless of the irrationality which characterizes much of their origins and practices. To such religious beliefs and practices, solving as they do the problem of how to behave successfully, we may apply the words which James uses in speaking of conversions: ". . . I there argued against the notion that the worth of a thing can be decided by its origin. Our spiritual judgment, I said, our opinion of the significance and value of a human event or condition, must be decided on empirical grounds exclusively. If the *fruits for life* of the state of conversion are good, we ought to idealize and venerate it, even though it be a piece of natural psychology; if not, we ought to make short work with it, no matter what supernatural being may have infused it."[73]

Applying these standards specifically to saintliness and its accompanying phenomena of asceticism, self-surrender, and mysticism, James declares that we should test saintliness by common sense, using "human standards to help us decide how far the religious life commends itself as an ideal kind of human activity." If the religious life produces good fruit, that is, if it produces behavior that brings man happiness, then "any theological beliefs that may inspire it, in so far forth will stand accredited."[74] If such beliefs do not lead to fruitful connections with the concrete problems of life, on the other hand, they are, by pragmatic and empirical principles, discredited.) It is quite possible, therefore, despite the attacks made on religion because of its "irrationality," to regard religion as both true and vitally necessary for man; indeed, the supernaturalism and optimism to which the hypotheses of mystical states would lead us may be the "truest of insights into the meaning of life."[75]

Unfortunately, many men reject all the contributions of religion because they find that mysticism does not fulfill rationalistic requirements, especially the rationalistic demand that our beliefs ought "ultimately to find for themselves articulate grounds." "Such grounds which the rationalist demands . . . must consist of four things: (1) definitely statable abstract principles; (2) definite facts of sensation; (3) definite hypotheses based on such facts; and (4) definite inferences logically drawn."[76] The ineffability of mystical experiences makes the satisfaction of such demands, of course, impossible; but James, following his own kind of empirical and pragmatic philosophy, rejects the criteria of rationalism, his own philosophy, as a matter of fact, vindicating the claims of saintly mysticism. As Royce says, "James reckons that the tribulations of religious doubts with which abstract scientific theories have beset our present age are not to be compared with the glory that perchance shall be, if only we open our eyes to what experience itself has to reveal to us."[77] (Reality, as we have seen, certainly exceeds logic and all formulas; this is true indeed with reference to mystical experiences. Here, as elsewhere, we always find that the "bottom of being is left *logically* opaque to us, as something which we simply come upon and find. . . ."[78] Approached, however, by non-rationalistic means, that is, by love, and faith, and self-surrender, this opaqueness of being, which logic can never pierce, is mysteriously and wonderfully penetrated.)

As we have already seen, in this chapter, one of the most urgent problems of our moral life, once we have established that there are ideals and that we should seek to actualize them, is the construction of a casuistic scale. Even when we *have* decided to do good, we face the additional problem of choosing which out of the many competing goods waiting for actualization shall be realized and which shall be sacrificed. The truly good life requires us to choose that good which is the most desirable of all available goods and, at the same time, destroys the smallest possible number of competing goods. We see the importance of making an intelligent decision in this matter when we understand that in choosing one good in preference to another good we are in effect choosing one moral universe and rejecting another set of moral goods.

As we have seen, this vitally important moral problem of constructing and choosing a satisfactory casuistic scale must be solved without the aid of abstract, *a priori* guiding principles. Spurning the pretentions of the rationalists, who claim to have satisfactory general principles, pragmatists look elsewhere for guidance; and, fortunately, they find it in the concrete experiences of mankind.

Examining the record of mankind's moral experiences, we discover as a matter of concrete fact that the most satisfactory casuistic scales, and, correspondingly, the most perfectly moral human lives, have been developed in connection with man's religious experiences. The record of Stoicism and of Epicureanism shows the emergence of noble casuistic scales, and history records the details of the noble lives of men who directed their conduct in terms of those scales. But experience also shows us the record of Christianity and other twice-born, non-naturalistic religions and discloses that these religions have been connected with the most satisfactory casuistic scale, and, in their saints, have produced men who were the most successful, morally speaking. In the case of all these religions, the casuistic scales and the inspiration to live according to them have emerged from mystical experience.

We now find that James's pragmatism and empiricism, strangely enough, look for the last and highest word on moral questions to the realm of mystical experiences. Actually, this is not strange at all, because the testimony of mystical experiences is to be tested by the same pragmatic and empiricist criteria which are used to test all other types of experiences; if they pass these tests, the truths of mystical knowledge must be allowed to take their place alongside all other verified truths. As James puts it, *"If the mystical truth that comes to a man proves to be a force that he can live by, what mandate have we of the majority to order him to live in another way?"*[79] The verification of mystically engendered truths, like that of all truths, lies in the fact that they originate in concrete experiences and in the fact that they place us in fruitful relation with reality. In the extensive record of mystical experiences we have proof that mystical knowledge has a truly experiential basis;[80] the ability of such knowledge to place us in fruitful relations with reality is seen by examining mysticism's casuistic scale and the effectiveness of the inspiration which mysticism provides to those who live in its light. This can be done by looking at the lives of good Christians, especially the lives of the saints.

First, however, we should briefly note a few of James's basic views about mysticism, specifically his answer to the question as to whether mystical experience furnishes any warrant for the truth of "the twice-bornness and supernaturality and pantheism which it favors."[81] James's answer regarding the authority of mystical experience is summed up in the following observations:

(1) Mystical states, when well developed, usually are, and have the right to be, absolutely authoritative over the individuals to whom they come.

(2) No authority emanates from them which should make it a duty for those who stand outside of them to accept their revelations uncritically.

(3) They break down the authority of the non-mystical or rationalistic consciousness, based upon the understanding and the senses alone. They show it to be only one kind of consciousness. *They open out the possibility of other orders of truth, in which, so far as anything in us vitally responds to them, we may freely continue to have faith.*[82]

Mysticism is the name used to describe the special manner in which truth is seen by religious persons.[83] To see mystical truths, one must have a spiritual orientation which is radically different from that of the non-mystical man. This orientation, or dedication, may come about as a result of a sudden or gradual process of conversion, but no matter how or when it appears in a man, it must involve the rejection of the world and the flesh and a deep absorption in and commitment to spiritual interests. To be thus absorbed and committed is to be twice-born, meaning that the mystic must die as far as the sensuous life is concerned and be reborn on the level of the spiritual.

A study of religions discloses that all religious creeds appear to agree in being concerned with "a certain uniform deliverance," which consists of two parts: (1) an uneasiness, making us feel that there is *"something wrong about us* as we naturally stand"; and (2) the solution of that uneasiness by a "sense that *we are saved from* the wrongness by making proper connections with the higher powers." In more highly developed minds, this wrongness takes a "moral character" and the salvation a "mystical tinge"; starting with the experience of his own "wrongness," the man moves on to a consciousness of a higher being, with which he is "conterminous," a being which sets that wrongness right.

The individual, so far as he suffers from his wrongness and criticises it, is to that extent consciously beyond it, and in at least possible touch with something higher, if anything higher exist. Along with the wrong part there is thus a better part of him, even though it may be but the most helpless germ. With which part he should identify his real being is by no means obvious at this stage; but when stage 2 (the stage of solution or salvation) arrives, the man identifies his real being with the germinal higher part of himself; and does so in the following way. *He becomes conscious that this higher part is conterminous [sic] and continuous with a more of the same quality, which is operative in the universe outside of him, and which he can keep in working touch with, and in a fashion get on board of and save himself when all his lower being has gone to pieces in the wreck.*[84]

Mystical experiences and the accompanying moral reorganization involve, therefore, the giving up of one's "natural life" and the participation in the larger spiritual life; the yielding up of one's personal will with its corresponding emphasis on the imperfect self; the discovery of unsuspected depths of character, lying below the levels known in the natural life; a complete and decisive change in one's center of energy, revealing the real meaning of one's experiences; and, finally, the disposition of the genuine child of God to serve with a permanently patient heart and to eradicate the love of self.

Mystical experiences and the moral life which they inspire are characterized by paradoxes which, like anything else proposed for our belief, can be validated only by pragmatic tests. When we are told, for example, that we can have abundant life only by going through the process of death and rebirth, we cannot know whether this is truth or fantasy; the answer must wait on the investigation of our experiences. If death and rebirth do put us into more fruitful connections with reality, the paradox is indeed true. Thus, by the same test it is true that it is wrong to hate our enemy; that we can realize ourselves only by renouncing ourselves; that we can save our souls only by losing them.[85] Pragmatically it is true also that "to give up one's conceit or hope of being good in one's own right is the only door to the universe's deeper riches."[86]

Like all other beliefs, those proposed for our acceptance by mystics are to be judged not by their *origins* but by their *results*. Pragmatism does not care where a truth comes from or how it originates. It really does not care, for example, whether it rests upon a theistic or an atheistic hypothesis. Thus, if a belief is shown to *work* when we apply it to our concrete problems it is true in the highest and only sense in which anything can be true. In this sense, many of the beliefs which have come out of mystical experiences are seen to be indeed true.

The success with which some mystical beliefs pass the pragmatic test, as contrasted with the corresponding failures of naturalistic beliefs, is shown in the resources which mysticism releases for man's moral life. Placing aside the "literal and legal virtues" of "naturalism," mystical experiences reveal "possibilities which take our breath away," possibilities of "another kind of happiness and power, based on giving up our will and letting something higher work for us"; mystical experiences seem to show "a world wider than either physics or philistine ethics can imagine."[87] Indeed, the world revealed by mystical knowledge and attained by mystical self-surrender is one in which "all is well, in *spite* of certain forms of death, indeed *because* of certain forms of death—death of hope, death of strength, death of responsibility . . . death of everything that paganism, naturalism, and legalism pin their faith on and tie their trust to."[88] The very thought of the divine order of reality yields the saint a "superior denomination of happiness, and a steadfastness of soul with which no other can compare."[89] In this happiness and steadfastness one finds the pragmatic verification of the claims of mysticism and saintliness.

This happiness which is the fruit of a saintly life faces

the facts of evil in the world with a realism that puts to shame the so-called realism of the rationalists and materialists. Far from being a mere feeling of escape, religious happiness looks directly into the face of evil; the mystic, with his moral life transformed, consents to evil outwardly as a form of sacrifice, knowing at the same time that, inwardly, evil has been permanently overcome. In his self-abandonment, the saint rests upon the providence of God, having sacrificed himself ruthlessly and recklessly; in the presence of God he finds that he has attained "the higher safety."[90] His higher happiness holds all lower happiness in check.

If we examine the records of saintly lives in a pragamtic way and ask what practical fruits such lives bear, we find that saintliness can be a "genuinely creative force, tending to make real a degree of virtue which it alone is ready to assume as possible."[91] Although we find that "saintliness of character may yield almost absolutely worthless fruits if it be associated with . . . inferior intellectual sympathies,"[92] it is also true that such splendid excellencies as felicity, purity, charity, patience, self-severity, are shown in "the completest possible measure"[93] in the lives of the saints. The saints are pragmatically justified in the moral realm by the very fact that they are "authors, auctores, increasers, of goodness."[94]

Further vindication of saintly conduct and ideals is found in the fact that "the general function of his [the saint's] charity in social evolution is vital and essential."[95] Moreover, the very fact that the saint and his own community are never fully adjusted to one another indicates that the ideal direction for changes in the community would be to move towards a general increase of saintliness. Saintliness as an ideal for society is discussed in the following passage:

> It is meanwhile quite possible to conceive an imaginary society in which there should be no aggressiveness, but only sympathy and fairness,—any small community of true friends

now realizes such a society. Abstractly considered, such a
society on a large scale would be the millenium, for every
good thing might be realized there with no expense of
friction. To such a millenial society the saint would be
entirely adapted. . . . The saint is therefore abstractly a
higher type of man than the "strong man," because he is
adapted to the highest society conceivable, whether that
society ever be concretely possible or not.[96]

In the saint we find that James discovers the apex of moral
perfection. In saintliness he finds the highest development so
far realized in the moral evolution of the world, an evolution
which is advanced by the cooperative efforts of God and
good men.

Notes

NOTES FOR CHAPTER ONE

1. Ralph Barton Perry, *The Thought and Character of William James* (Boston: Little, Brown, and Company, 1935), II, 575.

2. The successful adaptation to one's concrete problems, which is the pragmatic test of moral ideals, presupposes the right choice as one faces the choice of making the seen world or the unseen world our chief sphere of adaptation, and the consequent selection of aggressiveness or non-resistance as our means of adaptation. See William James, *The Varieties of Religious Experience* (New York: Longmans, Green, and Company, 1903), pp. 371-76.

3. Dietrich Von Hildebrand, *Christian Ethics* (New York: David McKay Company, Inc., 1955), p. 9.

4. *Ibid.,* p. 4.

5. William James, *The Will to Believe* (New York: Longmans, Green, and Co., 1927), p. 131.

6. *Ibid.,* p. 142.

7. *Ibid.,* p. 169.

8. *Ibid.,* p. 174.

9. *Ibid.,* p. 192.

10. *Ibid.,* p. 130.

11. *Ibid.,* pp. 194-95.

12. *Ibid.,* p. 201.

13. *Ibid.,* p. 193.

14. *Ibid.,* p. 197.

15. *Ibid.,* p. 109.

16. *Ibid.,* p. 107.

17. *The Varieties of Religious Experience,* p. 45.

18. *The Will to Believe,* p. 141.

NOTES FOR CHAPTER TWO

1. William James, *Some Problems of Philosophy* (London: Longmans, Green, and Co., 1948), p. vii.

2. Herbert W. Schneider, *A History of American Philosophy* (New York: Columbia University Press, 1946), p. 154.

3. "The Moral Philosopher and Moral Life," *The Will to Believe,* p. 210.

4. "The Sentiment of Rationality," *The Will to Believe,* p. 84.

5. The universe, we may say, must "fit" man's moral needs. Man is truly *in* and *of* the universe, and his needs are as real as any other data which are presented to us. It is as logical, therefore, in James's framework, to ask other types of data to be fitted to man's moral needs (and to be tested by them) as it would be to test moral data by other types of data. As we shall see, he will maintain that moral needs must be given priority in constructing our universe, that is, priority over other types of human demands.

6. *Ibid.,* pp. 82-83.

7. William James, *The Principles of Psychology* (New York: Dover Publications, 1950), II, 667.

8. "The Sentiment of Rationality," *The Will to Believe,* p. 93.

9. William James, *Letters of William James,* ed. Henry James (Boston: Atlantic Monthly Press, 1920), II, 296.

10. Morality and religion (that is, religion seen as the great transforming catalyst of the moral life) are really the central interests in James's thinking. Russell perceived this. "The three founders of pragmatism differ greatly *inter se;* we may distinguish James, Schiller, and Dewey as respectively its religious, literary, and scientific protagonists" (Bertrand Russell, *Sceptical Essays* [New York: Norton, 1928], p. 61).

11. William James, *Pragmatism* (New York: Meridian Books, 1955), p. 14.

12. *Letters,* II, 267. (Italics added.)

13. For a discussion of pragmatism as a theory of truth, see, *infra,* Chapter IV, "Epistemology and Morality."

14. Cf. Schneider, *History of American Philosophy,* p. 527. (". . . in 1897 . . . James . . . first referred to his point of view as

pragmatism . . .") ; Dewey, *Philosophy and Civilization* (New York: Minton, Balch & Company, 1931), p. 22 (". . . James was an empiricist before he was a pragmatist . . .").

15. Dewey, *Ibid.,* p. 22.

16. Charles Saunders Peirce, "Pragmatism," in *Collected Papers of Charles Saunders Peirce* (Cambridge: Harvard University Press, 1936), V, 276.

17. Morris R. Cohen, *American Thought: A Critical Sketch* (Glencoe, Illinois, The Free Press, 1954), p. 287. Since James came to an explicit avowal of pragmatism long after he had become a Radical Empiricist, Cohen's description of pragmatism as the vestibule of Empiricism is less than ideal. But his metaphor is not altogether inapt, inasmuch as it illustrates the close relationship, short of identity, which exists between the two. However, a more dynamic metaphor would probably be more suitable to their relationship.

18. So also for Peirce. "Pragmatism is a method in philosophy . . . It will be seen that *pragmatism* is not a *Weltanschauung* but a method of reflexion having for its purpose to render ideas clear." (Peirce, *Ibid.,* V, 9.)

19. Cf. *A Pluralistic Universe,* pp. 225-72. See also our Chapter IV, "Epistemology and the Moral Life."

20. Cf. *Some Problems of Philosophy,* p. 198 *et seq.* Hume's empiricism is the "most half-hearted" of all. For example, his treatment of causation is not an empirically inspired acceptance of the experienced facts but rather, says James, one of those "conceptual translations [which] always maltreat fact." (*Ibid.*)

21. In his insistence on acceptance of *all* experiences, James stands squarely in the American tradition of Emerson and Thoreau. Cf. ". . . a fact is an Epiphany of God." (Ralph Waldo Emerson, *Lectures and Biographical Sketches* [Boston: Houghton, Mifflin and Company, 1883], X, 132.) "If you stand right fronting and face to face to a fact, you will see the sun glimmer on both its surfaces, as if it were a cimeter [*sic*], and feel its sweet edge dividing you through the heart and marrow, and so you will happily conclude your mortal career. Be it life or death, we crave only reality. If we are really dying, let us hear the rattle in our throats and feel cold in the extremities; if we are alive, let us go about our business." (Henry David Thoreau, *Walden* [London: J. M. Dent & Sons Ltd., 1955], p. 88.)

22. *The Meaning of Truth,* p. 102.

23. *Some Problems of Philosophy*, p. 106.

24. *Ibid.*, pp. 198-200.

25. William James, *A Pluralistic Universe* (New York: Longmans, Green, and Co., 1909) , p. 252.

26. Compare with the words of Gabriel Marcel: "The given is truly a gift. Only reality is given, but it is fully given only in the act by which things are received and welcomed as presences." (In Henry G. Bugbee, Jr., *The Inward Morning: A Philosophical Exploration in Journal Form* [State College, Penna.: Bald Eagle Press, 1958], p. 27.)

27. William James, *The Meaning of Truth* (New York: Longmans, Green, and Co., 1909), p. xiii.

28. *Ibid.*, p. 92.

29. *Ibid.*

30. William James, *Essays in Radical Empiricism* (New York: Longmans, Green, and Co., 1947), p. 37.

31. James's theory of experience follows the modern trend of attempting to solve the problem of cognition by obliterating the separateness of subject and object. Sorokin reviews the history of this trend as follows: "Finally, the problem of an unmediated cognition of the object by the subject is one of the central problems of contemporary philosophy and epistemology. The attempts of Hume and Kant (of the *Critique of Pure Reason),* of Hegel and others to solve it without obliterating the "separateness" of subject and object have failed. . . . In different degrees and manners, . . . [many] thinkers seem to state that without an obliteration of the separateness of subject and object, no adequate cognition of the true reality is possible. And the obliteration seemingly cannot be accomplished through purely sensory perception and logic of intellect: some sort of direct intuition is necessary for that." (Pitirim A. Sorokin, *The Ways and Power of Love* [Boston: The Beacon Press, 1954], p. 367.)

32. "The Thing and Its Relations," in *Essays in Radical Empiricism*, p. 100. See, *infra,* Chapter IV, "Epistemology and Morality," for a detailed discussion of this problem.

33. *Ibid.*, p. 94.

34. *Ibid.*, p. 93.

35. Perry, *The Thought and Character of William James*, II, 391-92 (Perry is quoting James.).

36. *The Meaning of Truth*, p. 132.

37. *The Principles of Psychology*, II, 634.

38. "Reflex Action and Theism," *The Will to Believe*, p. 118.

39. *Some Problems of Philosophy*, p. 151.

40. *A Pluralistic Universe*, p. 286.

41. "The Dilemma of Determinism," *The Will to Believe*, p. 147.

42. "Reflex Action and Theism," *The Will to Believe*, p. 119.

43. Ralph Barton Perry, *In the Spirit of William James* (New Haven: Yale University Press, 1938), p. 105.

44. In approaching the problem of monism, dualism, and pluralism, James is guided by the rule that a philosopher should not consider at all any questions whose answers make no practical differences in human lives. Thus, he will not consider the question as to whether there is a world "beyond" this world, one which has no influence upon us or upon our world.

45. *Some Problems of Philosophy*, p. 127.

46. *Varieties of Religious Experience*, p. 137.

47. *A Pluralistic Universe*, p. 117.

48. *Varieties of Religious Experience*, p. 165.

49. *Ibid.*, p. 163.

50. James, *Letters*, I, 247.

51. *A Pluralistic Universe*, pp. 49-50.

52. *Ibid.*, p. 328.

53. *Letters*, I, 238.

54. William James, *The Literary Remains of Henry James*, (Boston: Houghton, Mifflin & Co., 1884), p. 115.

55. *A Pluralistic Universe*, p. 319.

56. *Ibid.*, p. 325.

57. *Ibid.*, p. 236.

58. *Ibid.*, p. 129.

59. *Ibid.*, p. 321.

60. James, "Syllabus of Philosophy 3" in Perry, *Thought and Character*, II, 747.

61. *Ibid.*, pp. 748-49.

62. Perry, *Thought and Character*, II, 382.

63. *Ibid.*, p. 73.

64. "The Dilemma of Determinism," *The Will to Believe*, pp. 161-62.

65. Radical Empiricism is not identical with pluralism, change, and chance in the sense that there is a necessary logical connection between them. As a matter of fact, if man's ex-

perience revealed a universe that was absolutely one and completely determined, Radical Empiricism would be monistic and deterministic. As it is, its pluralism is empiricist—not doctrinaire.

66. *A Pluralistic Universe*, p. 48.

67. *Ibid.*, p. 44.

68. *Ibid.*, p. 159.

69. "On Some Hegelisms," *The Will to Believe*, p. 270.

70. *Ibid.*, p. 294.

71. "The Dilemma of Determinism," *The Will to Believe*, p. 161.

72. *Ibid.*, p. 152.

73. "Is Life Worth Living?" *The Will to Believe*, p. 44. (Nature without man would be a moral nullity.)

74. "The Sentiment of Rationality," *The Will to Believe*, p. 104.

75. "Is Life Worth Living?" *The Will to Believe*, p. 44.

76. *Varieties of Religious Experience*, p. 492.

77. "Is Life Worth Living?" *The Will to Believe*, p. 52.

78. *Ibid.*, p. 43.

79. "The Sentiment of Rationality," *The Will to Believe*, p. 103.

80. "The Moral Philosopher and the Moral Life," *The Will to Believe*, p. 193.

81. "The Sentiment of Rationality," *The Will to Believe*, p. 103.

82. *Ibid.*, p. 102.

83. *A Pluralistic Universe*, p. 150.

84. "The Sentiment of Rationality," *The Will to Believe*, p. 104.

85. *Ibid.*, p. 106.

86. *Ibid.*, p. 102.

87. Mussolini, for example, said: "The pragmatism of William James was of great use to me in my political career. James taught me that an action should be judged by its results rather than by its doctrinary basis." (Quoted in Perry, *Thought and Character*, II, 575.) (The equivocation involved in using *pragmatism* to refer to the utterly divergent views of Mussolini and James will be discussed later.)

88. *Some Problems of Philosophy*, p. 221.

89. *Ibid.*, p. 229.

90. *A Pluralistic Universe*, p. 351.

91. *Some Problems of Philosophy,* p. 141.

92. This must not be understood to imply that James rejected *concepts* as such. While he rejected every vicious conceptualization of reality, he affirmed that concepts were as real as percepts and saw them as having an invaluable teleological character. See the discussion of concepts, *infra.*

93. "Is Life Worth Living?" *The Will to Believe,* p. 62.

94. "The Dilemma of Determinism," *The Will to Believe,* pp. 178-79.

95. See *infra,* p. 138.

96. *Some Problems of Philosophy,* p. 145.

97. Perry, *Thought and Character,* II, 664.

98. "The Dilemma of Determinism," *The Will to Believe,* p. 157.

99. *Some Problems of Philosophy,* p. 190.

100. *Ibid.,* p. 209.

101. *Ibid.,* p. 215.

102. "The Will to Believe," *The Will to Believe,* p. 28. James, like Dewey, has the intuition that man is *not* outside reality, not a spectator. Man is essentially and deeply related to the world.

103. *A Pluralistic Universe,* p. 318.

104. *Some Problems of Philosophy,* p. 225.

105. *Ibid.,* p. 142.

106. *Ibid.,* p. 223.

107. *Ibid.,* p. 230.

108. "Is Life Worth Living?" *The Will to Believe,* p. 61.

109. "The Sentiment of Rationality," *The Will to Believe,* p. 101.

110. "Is Life Worth Living?" *The Will to Believe,* p. 54.

111. *The Varieties of Religious Experience,* p. 519.

NOTES FOR CHAPTER THREE

1. *Varieties of Religious Experience,* p. 41.

2. James declares that "morality pure and simple" obeys the law with the "heaviest and coldest heart," but religion never finds the service of the highest to be a "yoke." (*Ibid.*)

3. William Bixler, *Religion in the Philosophy of William James* (Boston: Jones, 1926), p. 4. (Italics added.)

4. *Varieties of Religious Experience,* p. 39.
5. "Is Life Worth Living?" *The Will to Believe,* p. 42.
6. *A Pluralistic Universe,* p. 307.
7. *Ibid.,* p. 307.
8. *Ibid.,* p. 308. For his pansychic views James acknowledges a debt to Fechner; James believed that Fechner's ideas were "not without direct empirical verification." *(Ibid.)*
9. *Varieties of Religious Experience,* p. 58.
10. "Is Life Worth Living?" *The Will to Believe,* p. 52. (Italics have been added.)
11. *Varieties of Religious Experience,* p. 508.
12. "Is Life Worth Living?" *The Will to Believe,* p. 56.
13. *A Pluralistic Universe,* p. 33.
14. "Is Life Worth Living?" *The Will to Believe,* p. 57.
15. *Ibid.*
16. *Ibid.,* p. 55.
17. "Reflex Action and Theism," *The Will to Believe,* p. 120.
18. *Thought and Character,* I, 467.
19. *A Pluralistic Universe,* pp. 314-15.
20. Ralph Barton Perry, *Present Philosophical Tendencies* (New York: George Braziller, Inc., 1955), p. 246.
21. *A Pluralistic Universe,* p. 331.
22. *Present Philosophical Tendencies,* p. 268.
23. *Varieties of Religious Experience,* p. 377. The nature and value of saintliness are discussed in our chapter "Man's Moral Life."
24. *A Pluralistic Universe,* p. 306. (Italics have been added.)
25. *Varieties of Religious Experience,* p. 518.
26. *A Pluralistic Universe,* p. 306.
27. Josiah Royce, *William James and Other Essays on the Philosophy of Life.* (New York: The Macmillan Company, 1911), p. 39.
28. "The Will to Believe," *The Will to Believe,* p. 25.
29. *Ibid.,* p. 26.
30. *Varieties of Religious Experience,* p. 141.
31. *Ibid.,* p. 486. (Actually, the "postulates" of science and of religion are in no sense arbitrary. If we, moreover, were to reject the demands which they make upon us, we would be denying some of the most important claims of our experience, and our knowledge and our practical affairs would suffer gravely

as a result. These postulates are founded in experience and verified by their fruits in our lives.)

32. "The Will to Believe," *The Will to Believe,* p. 27.

33. "Is Life Worth Living?" *The Will to Believe,* p. 59.

34. "Reflex Action and Theism," *The Will to Believe,* pp. 131-32.

35. *Varieties of Religious Experience,* p. 505. The total absence of faith means personal collapse, which may take the form of pathological depression. Faith is verified by the fact that it is indispensable to life. "Believe in the infinite as common people do, and life grows possible again." (*Ibid.,* p. 184.)

36. *Ibid.,* p. 18.

37. *Ibid.,* p. 455.

38. *Varieties of Religious Experience,* p. 334.

39. "The Will to Believe," *The Will to Believe,* p. 26.

40. *Ibid.,* p. 24. (Even if faith did *not* create its own verification, it would still be pragmatically desirable to have religious beliefs. Citing Pascal's "wager," James points out that the option to believe or not amounts to a choice wherein one may lose a reasonable *finite loss* if religion turns out to be false or an *infinite gain* if it turns out to be true. Thus, the "odds" favor belief over non-belief. [*Ibid.,* pp. 5-6.])

41. *The Varieties of Religious Experience,* p. 487.

42. *Ibid.,* p. 491.

43. *Ibid.,* p. 504.

44. *Ibid.,* p. 437.

45. Perry, *Thought and Character,* I, 493.

46. *Varieties of Religious Experience,* p. 48.

47. *Ibid.*

48. *Ibid.,* p. 259.

49. *Ibid.,* pp. 380-81.

50. Perry, *Thought and Character,* II, 471.

51. *Ibid.*

52. James, *Letters,* II, 213.

53. Perry, *Present Philosophical Tendencies,* pp. 370-71.

54. Perry, *Thought and Character,* II, 493.

55. *The Varieties of Religious Experience,* p. 38. (Italics added.)

56. "Reflex Action and Theism," *The Will to Believe,* p. 127.

57. Compare the views of Royce; "As a fact, the will as well as the reason is a source of religious insight. No truth is a saving

truth—yes, no truth is a truth at all unless it guides and directs life. Therein I heartily agree with current pragmatism and with James himself." (Josiah Royce, *The Sources of Religious Insight,* [New York: Charles Scribner's Sons, 1912], p. 144.)

58. "Reflex Action and Theism," *The Will to Believe,* p. 127. Man, being *in* and *of* this world, experiences the universe in the push and pressure of events and in the heat of moral actions. Thus, when James says that God's existence is best demonstrated by "practical" or "pragmatic" evidence, he means *not* that God is "useful" to man, but rather that a superior kind of evidence for God's existence is given to man in actions which provide profound insights and in the hunger for moral fulfillment which all men experience (and which only God can satisfy).

59. *The Meaning of Truth,* p. x.

60. *Ibid.*

61. *Pragmatism,* pp. 61-62.

62. *Ibid.,* p. 61. (This willingness to conform to the demands of all experiences, when allied with James's belief that experience equals reality, provides a strong basis for the pragmatic and experiential theology which he desired to construct.)

63. *Ibid.,* p. 192.

64. *A Pluralistic Universe,* p. 309.

65. *Collected Essays and Reviews,* p. 128.

66. Josiah Royce, *William James,* p. 21.

67. "Is Life Worth Living?" *The Will to Believe,* p. 51.

68. *The Principles of Psychology,* I, 316.

69. "Reflex Action and Theism," *The Will to Believe,* p. 116. (According to the theory of the triadic and reflex pattern, a mind must first "get its impression from the object which it confronts; then define what that object is, and decide what active measures its presence demands; and finally react." *Ibid.,* p. 123.)

70. *Ibid.,* p. 134.

71. *Ibid.,* pp. 115-16.

72. Compare with Royce's statement: ". . . the insight to which your opinions appeal is indeed the insight of a real being who values, estimates, establishes, decides as concretely as you do, and who is therefore not only all wise, but possessed of a will. Your search for salvation is a seeking to adjust yourself to this supreme will." (Josiah Royce, *The Sources of Religious Insight* [New York: Charles Scribner's Sons, 1912] p. 159.)

73. "The Moral Philosopher and the Moral Life," *The Will to Believe*, p. 214. (Belief in God is not an arbitrary matter. Experientially, James finds belief *demanded* of us; we *"must"* postulate a divine thinker; our experiences will verify his existence.)

74. James's faithfulness to experience was praised by Husserl: "Husserl speaks with praise of James's brilliant observations in the province of the descriptive psychology of presentational experience, which not only did not lead to psychologism, but aided him in breaking away from the psychologistic point of view." (Marvin Farber, *The Foundation of Phenomenology* [Cambridge: Harvard University Press, 1943] p. 277.)

75. *Letters*, II, 269.

76. *A Pluralistic Universe*, p. 29.

77. *Pragmatism*, p. 26.

78. *A Pluralistic Universe*, p. 25.

79. *The Varieties of Religious Experience*, p. 330.

80. *A Pluralistic Universe*, p. 30.

81. *Ibid.*, p. 44.

82. William James, *Memories and Studies* (New York: Longmans, Green, and Co., 1912), p. 204.

83. *The Varieties of Religious Experience*, pp. 445-46.

84. Fundamentally, James is reacting here, as elsewhere, against alleged truths which are completely static, independent of experience, and unrelated to action.

85. *The Varieties of Religious Experience*, p. 447.

86. *Ibid.*, p. 448.

87. *Pragmatism*, p. 85.

88. Perry, *Present Philosophical Tendencies*, p. 248.

89. "Reflex Action and Theism," *The Will to Believe*, p. 122.

90. *The Varieties of Religious Experience*, pp. 516-17.

91. *Pragmatism*, p. 193.

92. "Reflex Action and Theism," *The Will to Believe*, p. 122.

93. *Ibid.*, p. 127.

94. *Ibid.*

95. *The Varieties of Religious Experience*, p. 517.

96. *Thought and Character*, I, 486.

97. "The Moral Philosopher and the Moral Life," *The Will to Believe*, p. 196.

98. *Pragmatism*, p. 57.

99. *The Varieties of Religious Experience*, p. 369.

100. "Is Life Worth Living?" *The Will to Believe,* p. 51.
101. *The Varieties of Religious Experience,* p. 474.
102. *Pragmatism,* p. 78.
103. *Ibid.,* p. 77.
104. "The Moral Philosopher and the Moral Life," *The Will to Believe,* p. 213. James's use of the word *infinite* in this text is a lapse from his general insistence on the finite nature of God.
105. *Pragmatism,* p. 78.
106. "The Moral Philosopher and the Moral Life," *The Will to Believe,* pp. 212-13.
107. *Ibid.,* p. 213.
108. Here again we see the importance of behavior as opposed to "mere" knowing.
109. *The Varieties of Religious Experience,* p. 489.
110. "Reflex Action and Theism," *The Will to Believe,* p. 141.
111. "The Moral Philosopher and Moral Life," *The Will to Believe,* pp. 213-14.
112. *The Varieties of Religious Experience,* p. 329 .
113. "The Moral Philosopher and Moral Life," *The Will to Believe,* p. 212.
114. *Ibid.*
115. *The Varieties of Religious Experience,* p. 519.
116. Alfred North Whitehead, *Religion in the Making* (New York: The Macmillan Company, 1930), p. 136.
117. *Ibid.,* p. 153.
118. *The Varieties of Religious Experience,* p. 505. Compare with St. Augustine: "And the happy life is this—to rejoice unto Thee, in Thee, and for Thee; this is it, and there is no other." (St. Augustine, *The Confessions,* X, XXII).
119. *The Varieties of Religious Experience,* p. 47.

NOTES FOR CHAPTER FOUR

1. This, of course, might be suspected from the very nature of James's pragmatism, which, as we know, maintains that behavior is the end of every sound philosophy.
2. Perry, *Thought and Character,* I, 555.
3. *Some Problems of Philosophy,* p. 198.
4. Perry, *Thought and Character,* I, 554.

5. *Some Problems of Philosophy,* p. 198.

6. *Ibid.,* p. 200.

7. Perry, *Thought and Character,* I, 553.

8. *Collected Essays and Reviews,* p. 100.

9. Perry, *Thought and Character,* I, 551.

10. Perry suggests the possibility that James, especially in his *Essays in Radical Empiricism,* does not succeed in distinguishing between Pure Experience and subjective or conscious experience. (*Ibid.,* II, 391).

11. *Radical Empiricism,* p. 23.

12. *The Meaning of Truth,* p. 91.

13. *Pragmatism,* p. 169. Here, of course, James agrees with Hume.

14. James's rejection of all transempirical "beings" does not mean that he denies the possible existence of an invisible world with which men may have real relations. He insisted that we should believe "our life to be fed at the breasts of the greater life, or individuality to be sustained by the greater individuality, which must necessarily have more consciousness and more independence . . ." (*A Pluralistic Universe,* p. 150.) Such an invisible world is to be regarded as dynamically related to man and not juxtaposed in a lifeless connection; man must not let "a great chasm" yawn between him and "all that is higher," nor let God become "a thin nest of abstractions." (*Ibid.,* 151.)

15. *Principles of Psychology,* II, 634.

16. John Dewey, *Experience and Nature* (New York: W. W. Norton & Company, Inc., 1929), p. 295.

17. *Principles of Psychology,* II, 639.

18. *The Meaning of Truth,* p. 69.

19. "The Moral Philosopher and the Moral Life," *The Will to Believe,* p. 189.

20. See our discussion of "necessary truths," *infra.,* pp. 122 *et seq.*

21. *Principles of Psychology,* II, 639. (Italics added.)

22. *Ibid.,* II, 636. (Italics added.)

23. *Principles of Psychology,* II, 620.

24. *Ibid.,* II, 619.

25. *The Meaning of Truth,* p. 80. (Italics added.)

26. *Radical Empiricism,* p. 33. (Italics added.)

27. *A Pluralistic Universe,* pp. 194-95.

28. *The Meaning of Truth,* p. 91.

29. *Ibid.*, p. 73.

30. *A Pluralistic Universe*, p. 212.

31. *The Varieties of Religious Experience*, p. 499.

32. *Ibid.*

33. "The Will to Believe," *The Will to Believe*, p. 14.

34. *Pragmatism*, p. 250.

35. *Ibid.*, p. 240.

36. "On Some Hegelisms," *The Will to Believe*, p. 271.

37. *Talks to Teachers*, p. 15.

38. *Ibid.*, p. 17.

39. *Radical Empiricism*, p. 3.

40. William James, *Talks to Teachers on Psychology* (New York: Henry Holt and Company, 1939), p. 16.

41. Perry, *Thought and Character*, I, 480.

42. *The Meaning of Truth*, XV.

43. Perry, *Thought and Character*, I, 485.

44. *Talks to Teachers*, p. 25.

45. "Reflex Action and Theism," *The Will to Believe* pp. 140-41.

46. *Ibid.*, p. 141.

47. *Talks to Teachers*, pp. 23-24.

48. *Ibid.*, p. 25.

49. "Reflex Action and Theism," *The Will to Believe*, p. 117.

50. The spiritual setting is provided by a kind of pan-psychism which was suggested by Fechner, in which "our individual persons on earth [are like] unto so many sense-organs of the earth's soul." (*A Pluralistic Universe*, p. 170.) In his Hibbert Lectures in 1909, James urged his hearers to give consideration to Fechner's views.

51. "Reflex Action and Theism," *The Will to Believe*, p. 114.

52. *Ibid.*, p. 125.

53. *Ibid.*, p. 114.

54. *A Pluralistic Universe*, p. 249.

55. "The Sentiment of Rationality," *The Will to Believe*, p. 85.

56. Compare with St. Anselm's doctrine of truth, wherein he distinguishes truths of statement, of thought, of will, of natural and rational actions, of the senses, and of the essence of things. ("Dialogue on Truth," I, 152-64).

57. *Principles of Psychology*, I, 8.

58. "Reflex Action and Theism," *The Will to Believe*, p. 125.

59. "The Sentiment of Rationality," *The Will to Believe,* p. 64.

60. *A Pluralistic Universe,* p. 320.

61. "The Sentiment of Rationality," *The Will to Believe,* p. 64.

62. *Ibid.,* p. 110.

63. *A Pluralistic Universe,* p. 112.

64. *Ibid.,* pp. 112-13.

65. "The Dilemma of Determinism," *The Will to Believe,* p. 174.

66. "The Sentiment of Rationality," *The Will to Believe,* p. 79.

67. *Ibid.,* pp. 75-76.

68. "The Will to Believe," *The Will to Believe,* p. 11.

69. *A Pluralistic Universe,* p. 176.

70. *The Meaning of Truth,* p. xii.

71. *Pragmatism,* p. 158.

72. The whole discussion of truth rests upon a postulate which man, in his demand for rationality, is entitled to make: "The postulate that there is truth, and that it is the destiny of our minds to attain it . . ." ("The Will to Believe," *The Will to Believe,* p. 12) .

73. "Practical" must not be understood in a narrow, utilitarian sense. A truth which, for example, leads a man to God or provides a new insight into morality is practical in James's sense.

74. *Pragmatism,* p. 54.

75. *Ibid.,* p. 147.

76. *The Meaning of Truth,* p. 100. (Italics added.)

77. *Pragmatism,* p. 139. (Italics added.)

78. *The Meaning of Truth,* p. 160.

79. *Pragmatism,* pp. 245-46.

80. This will necessitate a deeper penetration into the nature of 'experience.'

81. "The Will to Believe," *The Will to Believe,* pp. 14-15.

82. *Ibid.,* p. 12.

83. "The Moral Philosopher and the Moral Life," *The Will to Believe,* p. 199.

84. *The Meaning of Truth,* pp. v-vi.

85. *Ibid.,* p. 161.

86. *Ibid.,* p. 135.

87. *Ibid.,* p. vii.

88. *Ibid.,* p. 82.

89. *Ibid.,* p. 56.

90. *Ibid.,* p. 235.

91. *Ibid.,* pp. vi-vii.

92. *Pragmatism,* p. 140.

93. *The Meaning of Truth,* p. 52.

94. *Ibid.,* p. 60.

95. *Ibid.,* p. 58.

96. *Ibid.,* p. 70.

97. *Pragmatism,* p. 167.

98. Perry, *Thought and Character,* II, 635. (We must not forget, however, that the "inventions" are nature's inventions in the sense that the human mind which does the inventing is itself organic to the universe.)

99. "The Will to Believe," *The Will to Believe,* p. 24.

100. *Ibid.,* p. 23.

101. *Ibid.,* p. 25.

102. *Ibid.,* pp. 22-23.

103. "Surely knowing is only one way of interacting with reality and adding to its effect." (*The Meaning of Truth,* p. 96.)

104. Compare this with the views of Royce: "We know only that the highest Truth is already attained from all eternity in the Infinite Thought, and that in and for that Thought the victory that overcometh the world is once for all won." (Josiah Royce, *The Religious Aspect of Philosophy* [New York: Harper and Brothers, 1958], p. 478.)

105. *Pragmatism,* p. 167.

106. *Ibid.,* p. 237.

107. *The Meaning of Truth,* p. 79.

108. *Ibid.,* p. 80.

109. *Ibid.,* p. 60.

110. *Pragmatism,* p. 206.

111. *Ibid.,* pp. 206-7.

112. *Ibid.,* p. 207.

113. Perry, *Thought and Character,* I, 468.

114. *Ibid.,* I, 467.

115. *Some Problems of Philosophy,* p. 186. (Of course "concepts inwardly absurd" could not be true concepts in the Jamesian sense, but rather inert, static, deadly intellectualistic imitations of concepts. *Real* concepts could not be more or less

real than percepts—since they are all parts of experience—and could not be at odds with perception.)

116. *Ibid.,* pp. 78-79.

117. Perry, *Thought and Character,* I, 547-48. (However, in so far as a given concept is particular and concrete it is just as much opposed to the abstract and general as is any perception.)

118. *The Principles of Psychology,* II, 6.

119. *Ibid.,* II, 7.

120. *Some Problems of Philosophy,* p. 108.

121. *The Principles of Psychology,* II, 7.

122. *Ibid.,* II, 9.

123. *Ibid.,* II, 27.

124. *The Varieties of Religious Experience,* p. 445.

125. *A Pluralistic Universe,* pp. 89-90.

126. *Some Problems of Philosophy,* p. 71.

127. *Pragmatism,* p. 115.

128. *Some Problems of Philosophy,* pp. 64-66.

129. *Ibid.,* p. 200.

130. *The Meaning of Truth,* p. 43.

131. *A Pluralistic Universe,* p. 217.

132. *The Varieties of Religious Experience,* p. 57.

133. Perry, *Thought and Character,* I, 547.

134. *Radical Empiricism,* pp. 16-17.

135. Perry, *Thought and Character,* II, 663. (The words are Perry's own.)

136. *Some Problems of Philosophy,* p. 101.

137. *Ibid.*

138. *Ibid.,* p. 106.

139. *A Pluralistic Universe,* p. 251.

140. *Ibid.,* p. 235. (Italics added. The meaning of *practical* here, of course, is not narrow and utilitarian.)

141. The philosophical significance of concepts is seen in the fact that they are indispensable for the formulation of ethical norms and in the corresponding guidance of life in facing concrete moral problems.

142. *Some Problems of Philosophy,* p. 73.

143. *Ibid.*

144. *Ibid.,* p. 71.

145. *Varieties of Religious Experience,* p. 56.

146. *Some Problems of Philosophy,* p. 64.

147. *Pragmatism,* p. 114.

148. *A Pluralistic Universe*, p. 251.
149. *Ibid.*
150. *Some Problems of Philosophy*, p. 99.
151. *Ibid.*, p. 98.
152. *Ibid.*, p. 78. (Since reality is always growing, concepts, as presented by "vicious" intellectualism, distort reality with their static, unchanging contents.)
153. *A Pluralistic Universe*, p. 265.
154. *Ibid.*, p. 250.
155. *Ibid.*, p. 246.
156. *Ibid.*
157. *Ibid.*, p. 234.
158. *Ibid.*, p. 256.
159. *Ibid.*, p. 219.
160. *Ibid.*, p. 256.
161. *Ibid.*, pp. 218-19.
162. *Ibid.*, p. 60.
163. *Some Problems of Philosophy*, p. 102.
164. *The Will to Believe*, p. 70.
165. *A Pluralistic Universe*, p. 253.
166. *Ibid.*, pp. 248-49.
167. *Ibid.*, p. 248.
168. *Some Problems of Philosophy*, p. 74.
169. *Ibid.*, p. 27.
170. *Ibid.*, p. 62.
171. *Ibid.*, p. 58.
172. *Radical Empiricism*, p. 16.
173. *The Will to Believe*, pp. 119-20.
174. *Some Problems of Philosophy*, p. 52.
175. For James there can be no conflict between percepts and genuine concepts, that is, concepts seen as teleological instruments redirecting us fruitfully into concrete experience. However, there can be and are conflicts between perception and concepts as understood by vicious intellectualism and as seen in a falsely static universe.
176. *Ibid.*, p. 95.
177. *Pragmatism*, p. 173.
178. "The Sentiment of Rationality," *The Will to Believe*, p. 70.
179. "Reflex Action and Theism," *The Will to Believe*, p. 132. (Italics added.)

180. "The Will to Believe," *The Will to Believe,* p. 19.
181. *Ibid.,* p. 21.
182. *The Meaning of Truth,* p. 99.
183. *Ibid.*
184. "The Sentiment of Rationality," *The Will to Believe,* p. 92.
185. "The Will to Believe," *The Will to Believe,* p. 11.
186. "The Sentiment of Rationality," *The Will to Believe,* p. 83.
187. *Ibid.*
188. *The Varieties of Religious Experience,* pp. 501-2.
189. *Principles of Psychology,* II, 667. (Italics added.)
190. *The Varieties of Religious Experience,* p. 501.
191. "The Will to Believe," *The Will to Believe,* p. 21.
192. "Great Men and Their Environment," *The Will to Believe,* p. 253.
193. *Letters,* II, 270.
194. *Ibid.*
195. *The Principles of Psychology,* II, 634.
196. *Ibid.*
197. *Ibid.,* II, 640.
198. "The Sentiment of Rationality," *The Will to Believe,* p. 75. (We must understand that this mysteriousness must not be identified with an *unknowable* [such as Spencer's]; it is *knowable* in the sense that it calls for specific human responses.)
199. *Ibid.*
200. "On Some Hegelisms," *The Will to Believe,* p. 271.
201. "The Sentiment of Rationality," *The Will to Believe,* p. 93.
202. *The Meaning of Truth,* p. 90.
203. James admits one exception to this otherwise universal rule: there is one "indefectibly certain truth," namely, "the truth that the present phenomenon of consciousness exists." This truth, however, is only a mere admission of a stuff to be philosophized about. ("The Will to Believe," *The Will to Believe,* pp. 14-15.)
204. *Ibid.,* pp. 15-16.
205. *Ibid.,* p. 14.
206. *Ibid.,* p. 17.
207. *The Meaning of Truth,* p. 7.

208. "The Sentiment of Rationality," *The Will to Believe,*
p. 93.

209. *Pragmatism,* p. 177.

210. "The Will to Believe," *The Will to Believe,* p. 17.

211. *Letters,* II, 49.

212. "The Will to Believe," *The Will to Believe,* p. 17.

213. *Some Problems of Philosophy,* pp. 25-26. (Italics added.)
(On the other hand, philosophy is by no means bound to
accept the positivistic assumptions of some scientists; philosophy
is to devote itself to defending the existence of beings which
are beyond the ken of positivistic sciences.)

214. "The Will to Believe," *The Will to Believe,* p. 27.

215. "The Sentiment of Rationality," *The Will to Believe,*
p. 93.

216. *Ibid.,* p. 95.

217. *Some Problems of Philosophy,* p. 224.

218. "The Sentiment of Rationality," *The Will to Believe,*
p. 90.

219. *Some Problems of Philosophy,* p. 224.

220. *A Pluralistic Universe,* p. 329.

221. "The Will to Believe," *The Will to Believe,* p. 27.

222. *A Pluralistic Universe,* pp. 328-29.

223. "Reflex Action and Theism," *The Will to Believe,* pp.
116-17.

224. See (2), *supra.*

225. "The Will to Believe," *The Will to Believe,* p. 25.

226. *The Varieties of Religious Experience,* p. 377.

227. *Ibid.,* p. 375.

228. The problem of deciding between the competing claims
of various goods will be examined in detail in the next chapter
in another context, that of the casuistic problem. Regarding
Mussolini's pragmatism, we have this statement attributed to
him: "The pragmatism of William James was of great use to me
in my political career. James taught me that an action should
be judged rather by its results than by its doctrinary basis."
(Perry, *Thought and Character,* II, 575.)

229. "Reflex Action and Theism," *The Will to Believe,* p. 131.

230. *The Principles of Psychology,* II, pp. 617-78.

231. *Ibid.,* II, pp. 627-28.

232. *Ibid.,* II, 626.

233. *Ibid.*
234. *Ibid.,* II, 641. (In saying that *experience* has nothing to do with the genesis of pure sciences, James provides us with an instance of the ambiguous way in which he uses that word. Actually, they *are* products of experience.)
235. *Ibid.,* II, 634.
236. *Ibid.,* II, 639.
237. *Ibid.*
238. *Ibid.*
239. *Ibid.,* II, 640.
240. *Ibid.*
241. James affirms his "logical realism" in the following words: "What I am affirming here is the platonic [*sic*] doctrine that concepts are singulars, that concept-stuffs are inalterable, and that physical realities are constituted by various concept-stuffs of which they 'partake.' . . . The present book, which treats concrete percepts as primordial and concepts as of secondary origin, may be regarded as somewhat eccentric in its attempt to combine logical realism with an otherwise empiricist mode of thought." (*Some Problems of Philosophy,* p. 106.)
242. *The Meaning of Truth,* p. 101.
243. "Reflex Action and Theism," *The Will to Believe,* p. 117.
244. *The Meaning of Truth,* pp. 83-84.
245. *The Principles of Psychology,* II, 672.
246. *Ibid.*
247. *Ibid.*
248. "Reflex Action and Theism," *The Will to Believe,* p. 131.
249. *The Principles of Psychology,* II, 630-31.

NOTES FOR CHAPTER FIVE

1. "Reflex Action and Theism," *The Will to Believe,* pp. 141-42.
2. *Pragmatism,* p. 191.
3. *Ibid.* (Italics added.)
4. *Ibid.*
5. Gordon H. Clark, *Thales to Dewey,* (Boston: Houghton, Mifflin Company, 1957), p. 504.
6. *Pragmatism,* p. 191. (The ideal order is not *given* to man or *found* by him. Rather, the world which man "finds" is a

chaos; out of that chaos he *constructs* an ideal order by a deliberate selection of data that are morally relevant.)

7. "The Dilemma of Determinism," *The Will to Believe,* p. 165.

8. *Ibid.*

9. *Pragmatism,* p. 184.

10. "The Moral Philosopher and Moral Life," *The Will to Believe,* p. 193.

11. "Is Life Worth Living?" *The Will to Believe,* p. 61.

12. "The Sentiment of Rationality," *The Will to Believe,* p. 105. (James's position is definitely opposed to any "situational ethics." In the norms provided by some of the necessary ideas and by the standards of one's community, a man has criteria for evaluating all situations in terms of general principles.)

13. *The Meaning of Truth,* p. 90.

14. *Pragmatism,* p. 185.

15. *Letters,* II, 270. Like everything else, the moral absolute itself is undergoing a process of development, taking its chances, so to speak, with all other things. That it will evolve successfully depends to a large extent upon our *faith* in the emergence of a melioristic universe and in our cooperation with other beings who are working for a better world.

16. Josiah Royce, *William James and Other Essays on the Philosophy of Life,* p. 40.

17. *Ibid.*

18. Perry, *Thought and Character,* I, 488.

19. "Essays in Popular Philosophy," *The Will to Believe,* p. 174.

20. *Ibid.,* pp. 174-75.

21. *Talks to Teachers,* p. 187.

22. "The Moral Philosopher and Moral Life," *The Will to Believe,* p. 199.

23. *Ibid.,* p. 195.

24. "The Dilemma of Determinism," *The Will to Believe,* p. 174.

25. "The Will to Believe," *The Will to Believe,* pp. 22-23.

26. *The Principles of Psychology,* II, 672.

27. "The Moral Philosopher and Moral Life," *The Will to Believe,* p. 187.

28. *Ibid.,* p. 198.

29. *Ibid.*, p. 201.

30. "The Importance of Individuals," *The Will to Believe,* p. 258.

31. *The Principles of Psychology,* II, 672.

32. "Great Men and their Environment," *The Will to Believe,* p. 232.

33. *The Varieties of Religious Experience,* p. 328.

34. "Is Life Worth Living?" *The Will to Believe,* p. 61.

35. *The Varieties of Religious Experience,* p. 374.

36. *Ibid.*, p. 357.

37. *Talks to Teachers,* p. 189.

38. For example, a belief such as the one described as follows: "Be not afraid of life. Believe that life is worth living, and your belief will create the fact." ("Is Life Worth Living?" *The Will to Believe,* p. 62.)

39. *The Varieties of Religious Experience,* p. 55.

40. *Ibid.*, p. 261.

41. *Talks to Teachers,* p. 64.

42. *The Varieties of Religious Experience,* p. 264.

43. *Ibid.*, p. 487.

44. *Ibid.*

45. *Ibid.*, p. 170.

46. *Ibid.*, p. 175.

47. *Ibid.*, p. 194.

48. *Ibid.*, p. 239.

49. *Letters,* I, 148.

50. However, as we see in the following passage, ideas do play a role in so far as they provide us with useful means of directing us in dealing with experiences:

"Thus are your pupils to be saved; first, by the stock of ideas with which you furnish them; second, by the amount of voluntary attention that they can exert in holding to the right ones, however unpalatable; and third, by the several habits of acting definitely on these latter to which they have been severally trained."
(*Talks to Teachers,* p. 188.)

51. *The Varieties of Religious Experience,* p. 354.

52. *The Meaning of Truth,* pp. 149-50. (At this point one may observe that James expresses a somewhat narrow concept of prudence.)

53. "The Moral Philosopher and Moral Life," *The Will to Believe*, p. 203. (Italics added.)

54. *Ibid.*, p. 211

55. *Ibid.*, p. 205.

56. *Ibid.*, pp 209-10.

57. *Ibid.*, p. 209.

58. *Ibid.*, p. 210.

59. *Ibid.*, p. 206.

60. *Ibid.*

61. *Ibid.*

62. *Ibid.*, p. 207. (As a point of actual fact, James conceives moral judgments as not waiting exclusively in each and every case on the outcome of specific actions. One can, and should, be guided also by relevant necessary ideas and by the norms established by human experience.)

63. *Ibid.*, p. 208.

64. *Ibid.*

65. *Ibid.*, p. 214.

66. *The Varieties of Religious Experience*, p. 42.

67. *Ibid.*, pp. 143-44. (The pagans, never having died to the world and been reborn to the spirit, were, according to James, "once-born" men, as opposed to the "twice-born" Christians, Mohammedans, etc. As "once-born men," they inevitably became "unmitigated pessimists" [*Ibid.*, p. 142], and their souls accordingly became "world-sick.")

68. *Ibid.*, pp. 142-43.

69. *Ibid.*, p. 44.

70. *Ibid.*, p. 41.

71. *Ibid.*, p. 46.

72. ". . . behavior is the aim and end of every sound philosophy" ("Reflex Action and Theism," *The Will to Believe*, p. 142.)

73. *The Varieties of Religious Experiences*, p. 237.

74. *Ibid.*, p. 331.

75. *Ibid.*, p. 428.

76. *Ibid.*, p. 73.

77. Royce, *William James*, p. 23.

78. "The Sentiment of Rationality," *The Will to Believe*, p. 73. (Italics added.)

79. *The Varieties of Religious Experience*, p. 423. (Italics added.)

80. James has no doubts about the validly experiential nature

of authentic mystical experiences (authenticity being tested, of course, by their fruits). He expresses his views very definitely in *The Varieties of Religious Experience*. The following lines are representative: "Our own more 'rational' beliefs are based on evidence exactly similar in nature to that which mystics quote for theirs. Our senses, namely, have assured us of certain states of fact; but mystical experiences are as direct perceptions of fact for those who have them as any sensations ever were for us." (*The Varieties of Religious Experience*, pp. 423-24.)

81. *Ibid.*, p. 422. James declares that the unanimity of the mystics is "far from being strong." They variously favor asceticism and antinomian self-indulgence, theism and pantheism. But these divergencies refer only to the intellectual expressions regarding their experiences; they all agree in the experience of the mystical feeling of *enlargement, union,* and *emancipation.* This feeling has "no specific intellectual content whatsoever of its own." (*Ibid.*, pp. 424-25.)

82. *Ibid.*, pp. 422-23. (Italics added.)

83. This special way of seeing the truth is, however, only one aspect of mysticism. James proposes, in addition, three other characteristic marks: ineffability, transiency, and passivity. (*The Varieties of Religious Experience*, pp. 380-82.)

84. *Ibid.*, p. 508. In a footnote relative to this passage James declares that the stage of salvation may arrive for some men gradually or suddenly, while others "practically enjoy it all their life." (*Ibid.*)

85. *A Pluralistic Universe*, p. 99.

86. *Ibid.*, p. 305.

87. *Ibid.*

88. *Ibid.*, pp. 305-6.

89. *The Varieties of Religious Experience*, p. 369.

90. *Ibid.*, p. 321.

91. *Ibid.*, p. 357.

92. *Ibid.*, p. 346.

93. *Ibid.*, p. 370.

94. *Ibid.*, p. 357.

95. *Ibid.*, p. 358.

96. *Ibid.*, p. 375.

Index